REAL TALES
of REAL DOGS

By
ALBERT PAYSON TERHUNE

Etchings by
DIANA THORNE

Albert Payson Terhune

Albert Payson Terhune was born on 21st December 1872, in New Jersey, United States. Terhune's father was the Reverend Edward Payson Terhune and his mother, Mary Virginia Hawes, was a writer of household management books and pre-Civil War novels under the name Marion Harland. He was one of six children, having four sisters and one brother, but only two of his sisters survived until adulthood. Further tragedy beset the family when his own wife, Lorraine Bryson Terhune, died four days after giving birth to their only child. He later remarried Anice Terhune, but had no more children.

Terhune received a Bachelor of Arts degree from Columbia University in 1893. The following year, he took a job as a reporter at the New York newspaper *The Evening World*, a position he held for the next twenty years. During this period, he began to publish works of fiction, such as *Dr. Dale: A Story Without A Moral* (1900), *The New Mayor* (1907), *Caleb Conover, Railroader* (1907), and *The Fighter* (1909). However, it was his short stories about his collie Lad, published in *Red Book*, *Saturday Evening Post*, *Ladies' Home*

Journal, *Hartford Courant*, and the *Atlantic Monthly*, that brought him mainstream success. A dozen of these tales were collected in to novel form and released as *Lad: A Dog* in 1919. This was a best-seller and in 1962 was adapted into a feature film. He went on to produce over thirty novels focussing on the lives of dogs and enjoyed much success in the genre.

Terhune's interest in canines was by no means restricted to fiction. He became a celebrated dog-breeder, specialising in rough collies, lines of which still exist in the breed today. Sunnybank kennels were the most famous collie kennels in the United States and the estate is now open to the public and known as Terhune Memorial Park. Terhune died on 18th February 1942 and was buried at the Pompton Reformed Church in Pompton Lakes, New Jersey.

Contents

	Page
Aeroplane, the Dog who Turned Wolf	11
Satan, the War Dog	15
Abdul Hamid, the Dog who Was Not	18
A Nameless Mongrel, who Repaid a Kindness	22
Flash, Pointing a Mile-Distant Pheasant	23
Wotan, the Police Dog who Fought a Leopard	27
Roger, the Church-Going Bloodhound	30
Grip, the Eighteenth Century Canine Thief	34
Halil, the Saluki Hero of a Strange Contest	38
Wolf, Our Great Little Collie	41
Vigi, the Hero Dog of the Vikings	45
Mafeking, a War Dog of South Africa	49
Wallace, Glasgow's Immortal Fire Dog	52
Bobbie, the Three-Thousand-Mile Collie	56
Sport, a Battle with Wolves for a Baby's Life	59
Karroo, the Terrier Named for a Desert	63
Lory the Lurid, a Right Disreputable Dog	66
Rex, Missing for Six Weeks	70
Gengisk, the Dog who Saved a King	72
Fang, the Seventeenth Century Dog Detective	75
Pegeen, the Dog who Learned to Reason	79
Trick, a Lurcher with a Queer History	82
Hector, the Mischief Dog	86
Paddy, a Mongrel, but a Great Little Dog	89

Etchings

	Page
Prince of Wails	*Frontispiece*
Stream Line / Police Patrol	16
Old Gentleman Joe	24
Big Boy / The Tail of Hoffman	30
"Rats!" / Salukis	38
Jules	46
"Pistache"	52
Caught or Found? / Junior League Committee	56
Social Climbers	64
Great Dane / Setter Retrieving Pheasant	72
The Inconsolable	80
The Weather Bureau	86

Real Tales of Real Dogs

AEROPLANE

The Dog Who Turned Wolf

AEROPLANE was a beautiful young collie, lustrously black of coat, with white chest and paws and with splashes of tan on his cheeks and over his eyebrows—what is known technically as a "tri-color." He belonged to Mrs. Lunt of the Alstead Collie Kennels in Rahway, New Jersey. She had bred and raised him and carried him to his championship.

He was one of the finest looking collies I have seen. But he was also the most listless and, to outward appearances, the most stupid. I used to watch him by the hour, wondering at his lack of any of the fire and dash and quaint humor that are such essential parts of collie nature. He seemed to me dull and not interested in anything or anybody.

Yet he was not stupid. Underneath all his apathy he had queer traits that showed not only a brain but a power of reasoning. For example:

In the Alstead kennels there were many finely appointed yards or runways, each containing one or more thoroughbred collies. The door of each yard was securely fastened. Aeroplane used to work away at the fastening of his yard door, no matter how tightly it might be in place or how often one kind of fastening was changed for another. He would work away at it until it came undone. Then he would let himself out of his yard and into the general kennel enclosure, and so on to the fields beyond. But this was only half—the lesser half—of his odd achievement at jail-breaking.

The Dog Who Turned Wolf

In some yards were dogs he liked — gentle and playful young dogs that were his friends and playfellows. In other yards were dogs he did not like. The moment he was out of his own runway he would gallop across to the various yards of the dogs that were his friends, and he would unfasten the catch on each of the yard doors which confined his chums. Never by any chance would he let out any of the dogs he did not like. With the band of chosen pals he had set free, he would romp or ramble until he and they were caught and put back into their yards. Again and again Aeroplane would do this clever bit of jail-delivery, always choosing what dogs he would release and what dogs he would not.

Soon after he won his championship, Aeroplane was sold by Mrs. Lunt to Alex Donaldson, a young Canadian collie-fancier. The price was high for such a man to pay. Donaldson got credit for part of the sum. He took Aeroplane to his house on the outskirts of Toronto and fastened him in a specially prepared yard.

But Donaldson did not know Aeroplane's genius as a door-opener. A few hours later he went out to bring the new collie his dinner. The yard door was wide open. The yard was empty. Aeroplane had let himself out and had run away. With him had run away more tied-up investment than Donaldson could spare.

Search was made everywhere for the valuable missing dog. There was no sign of the runaway. Donaldson was unhappy on his own account, but he was unhappier on Aeroplane's. The young dog was adrift somewhere in the Canada countryside, with the formidable northern winter coming on.

Aeroplane had never learned how to forage for food. He had never caught so much as a mouse. From babyhood his meals had been handed

The Dog Who Turned Wolf

to him on a plate—a carefully balanced ration. From babyhood he had slept in his snug kennel house. He had had no experience with such ordinary woodland rambles as fall to the lot of most dogs.

What chance could such a dog have when he was turned loose in the winter wilderness, with neither food nor shelter provided for him? When all search proved vain, Donaldson decided the unfortunate collie must have starved to death, out in the snowy forests and hills.

But that was just what Aeroplane had *not* done. Thrown on his own resources and with no experience to guide him, the pampered "hothouse" dog had turned wolf. At least, he had gone straight back to the wolfish ways of his long-dead ancestors. Hereditary instinct came to his aid when human care was absent.

He fled to the woods. There he found an overgrown and disused dance platform in what had once been a picnic grove. The lattice work on one side of this platform had rotted away. Aeroplane crawled under and made the place his lair. This was his headquarters for almost a year thereafter. Here he slept by day, on a bed of dead leaves. At night he would sally forth on foraging expeditions. Mind you, he had never in his life caught so much as a mouse. Now when the average dog seizes a chicken, you can hear the noise for a mile, but foxes and wolves and coyotes have the strange art of killing in silence.

Aeroplane learned to creep into a henhouse and to seize and bear off the fattest fowls without their uttering a single squawk. Unless a hencoop door was actually locked, he managed to get it open and to rob the roosts. He learned the art of catching rabbits and birds. He lived on the fat of the land, taking toll from both forest and farms. His listlessness departed. His narrow frame filled out with mighty muscles. His coat was a marvel of thickness and lustre.

The Dog Who Turned Wolf

Early one morning he made the mistake of tackling a goat, larger than himself. Here was something he could not slay in silence. The din of warfare brought people to the spot, just as Aeroplane was killing the goat. The collie fled, with the humans close behind him. He had no time to double on his tracks or otherwise to confuse the trail. There was enough snow on the ground for his pursuers to track him to his lair.

Donaldson was notified. On his arrival he crawled under the platform. After a hard fight he captured the dog and led him home, confining him in a high stockade. For three days Aeroplane stood there, trembling, with head and tail adroop. Then all at once he became a civilized dog again, devoted to his master.

He swept the Canadian dog shows, quickly won his international championship and was acclaimed the greatest collie in all the Dominion. Donaldson got back his purchase money, several times over, during the next year or two of the champion's glorious career.

I wonder if any dog but a collie is close enough to the primitive to have turned wolf for a year and then to have turned back to being a dog again.

SATAN
The War Dog

THIS is the story of a black mongrel whose color and odd appearance won him the name of Satan. He was perhaps the most famous of the hundreds of highly trained messenger dogs on the western front during the war.

The French war-dogs were divided, roughly, into two classes: the "estafettes" and the "liaison" dogs. An estafette was trained to carry a message to some specified point. His work was comparatively simple, but the liaison dog must not only carry such messages, but must then return, with or without an answer, to his point of starting.

Satan was a liaison dog, and he did his most spectacular work at the siege of Verdun. It was at Verdun, by the way, that seventeen human couriers in succession were picked off by German fire and killed during their task of carrying messages, while a single liaison dog was clever enough to make the same trip with dispatches six or seven times before he was shot.

Near Verdun was a village which it was most important for the French to hold as it was the key to other positions. They garrisoned it with a few hundred men whose commandant had orders to hold it until reinforcements should relieve them. The village was as important to the Germans as to the French. A German detachment got around to the rear of it, enveloping the little town and cutting it off from all probability of aid. Day after day the garrison defended the place as best they might against the terrific German bombardment.

Then the Germans planted a battery on a hill to their left that

The War Dog

commanded the village, and hurled an avalanche of shells into the besieged huddle of houses. The defenders' ammunition was running low. Unless that battery on the hill at the left could be silenced, the village would be wiped out and its garrison with it. If only the main body of the French army could know of the battery's existence and hammer it with long-range guns, the village might be saved.

The telephone and telegraph were out of commission. The last carrier pigeon was dead. No human could carry the news to headquarters through that murderous enemy fire. The garrison had one hope, and one only. If, by any chance, headquarters should manage to get some message to them by means of a liaison dog, they could use the same dog to carry back news of their desperate condition, telling also the position of the German battery and begging for relief.

Then word was brought to the commandant by a sentinel that a jet black dog was rushing toward the village, from the direction of headquarters. The commandant looked through his field glasses at the distant speck that was moving rapidly in his direction. He saw it was the famous black Satan. The dog was coming along at a terrific pace, running with a queerly elusive gait that made him a difficult mark for the enemy sharpshooters. He was wearing a hideous gas mask, and seemed to have a fantastic-looking pair of wings on his shoulders.

As the commandant watched, Satan lurched sideways and crashed to the ground. A German bullet had found him. He staggered to his feet, reeling and dizzy. For an instant he seemed to have lost his way. Then he settled into that steady run again, heading for the village, with those odd wings flapping wildly from his shoulders. Another bullet reached him, cracking the bone of one of his legs. On three legs he limped at his best speed toward his destination.

Stream Line — Diana Thorne

Police Patrol — Diana Thorne

The War Dog

Presently he reached the village. Soldiers picked up the wounded and exhausted dog and carried him to the commandant. Then it was seen that the "wings" were two tiny wicker baskets, each containing a fluttering and scared carrier pigeon.

On Satan's collar the commandant found a scribbled message rolled up inside a brass tube. The message was from headquarters, promising to relieve the village on the following day, and bidding its stricken garrison to hold on until then. But, almost devoid of ammunition and with that German battery on their left showering them constantly with death, there seemed scant hope of being able to hold the village for an entire day longer.

The commandant wrote in a few words their fearsome situation, describing the position of the German battery. He wrote on thin paper and rolled it into a metal quill which he fastened to one of the carrier pigeons Satan had brought. He made a copy of the message and fastened it to the other pigeon, on the chance that one of the two might be brought down by a sharpshooter. Then he set free both pigeons, and the birds started back toward headquarters.

But the Germans had been on the lookout for such a move. A hundred sharpshooters began to blaze away at the birds. One of them was shot down before it had traveled a quarter mile. But the other pigeon kept on, unhurt.

An hour later the earth was shaken by the thunder of the French long-range guns, pounding the German battery to flinders. The village was saved—thanks to the pluck and wisdom and loyalty of a black mongrel dog named Satan.

ABDUL HAMID
The Dog Who Was Not

IT WAS in 1893. I was in Damascus, and just starting with my small caravan southward through Syria toward the Dead Sea and the Land of Moab. On my way to camp, to begin the journey, I rounded a corner and came upon a wholesale dog fight.

A bone-thin little gray-and-white dog was crouched in an angle of a wall, trying to fight off a dozen larger curs. A group of native Syrian boys were laughing and egging on the assailants. The poor little chap was bleeding and panting. He had not a chance to survive. Yet he was battling right pluckily against terrible odds.

My dragoman explained to me afterwards how the fight must have started. In those days, in Damascus as in Constantinople and in many another Near-East city, the dogs were the principal scavengers. Nobody owned these dogs, for to the Mohammedans a dog is an unclean animal whose mere touch is a defilement. But they were allowed to live because of their value as scavengers. Thus, each ward of the city had its own pack of scavenger dogs that kept alive by eating offal and garbage.

Each pack of dogs kept closely to its own district or quarter. If a dog from one ward should happen to stray over to another ward, then all the curs in the second ward would pitch onto him and kill and eat him. It was a real case of "dog eat dog," with no mercy asked or expected. So some of the street boys used to amuse themselves by catching a dog of one ward and carrying him over into the next ward, for the fun of seeing the latter ward's dogs pile onto him and kill him. They had a pretty sense of humor, hadn't they?

The Dog Who Was Not

This young dog I am telling you about was such a victim. Had my dragoman and myself arrived two minutes later, the onrushing curs must have gotten him down and torn his throat out. As it was, the little fellow's desperate courage appealed to me.

It was an insanely foolish thing, in those days, for a foreigner to interfere with the sport or the other activities of natives. Had I been older, I should have realized that and I should have gone on, paying no heed to the impending slaughter. But I was not quite twenty-one years old, and fond of dogs. So I jumped in among the pack of curs, laying about with my riding whip, till I cleared a way to the bravely battling little dog. I picked him up and bore him away. The street boys raised an outcry. My dragoman averted the danger of a crowd collecting by pitching a handful of small copper coins to the lads.

As soon as we were clear of the streets I set the dog down and walked on. He had snuggled quietly in my arms and had made no effort to escape. As I set him down, he followed me. My dragoman tried to drive him back. It was no use. He followed me to camp. There, to the disgust of the native servants, I fed him. He ate ravenously.

When we set off on our long horseback journey southward, he elected himself my chum and guard. All day long, in sun or rain, he would jog alongside my horse. All night he would lie in the doorway of my tent. Under the new influence of all the food he wanted, he lost his wolflike gauntness and became a good-looking enough animal.

I undertook to teach him a very few simple tricks, at such times as we were resting. To my surprise, I found he was more quick to learn them than any other dog I have seen. The natives would stand in wondering and muttering groups, watching him shake hands or lie down or roll over or "speak," at command. To them, it must have seemed

The Dog Who Was Not

miraculous. Perhaps never before had any of them heard of a trick dog.

He would let nobody enter my tent or come within six feet of me, unless first I told him it was all right. He was a good little pal and a mighty good little watchdog. Both these traits were the more peculiar, since none of his ancestors for centuries had served either as guard or as comrade for mankind.

Then one day, just a few miles north of the garrison town of Nablous, I made a fool of myself at his expense. It happened in this way.

I was sitting in the doorway of my tent at sunset, the dog at my feet. I called across to my dragoman:

"I'm going to name this puppy 'Abdul Hamid,' in honor of your illustrious Sultan. By tomorrow I'll have taught him to answer to his new name."

The dragoman did not accord to my silly remark the polite native smile which was his wont. Indeed, he seemed not to hear me. I glanced about. Every groom and muleteer was staring wide-eyed at me. To impress them, I made the puppy go through some more of his tricks.

Next morning, when I woke, the little dog was not lying at the tent door, where he belonged. I called to one of the muleteers and asked him where the dog was. He blinked owlishly and asked:

"What dog, *Howaji*? I have seen no dog."

I made the same inquiry of the camp cook and of my groom. Both stared in the same uncomprehending way and declared they had never seen any dog around our camp. This sort of thing was beginning to get on my nerves. I sent for my dragoman, and took him out of earshot of the others. Then, crossly, I demanded what everyone meant by saying there was no camp dog.

My dragoman was a wise man, and I think he had grown to like

The Dog Who Was Not

me during our long months of riding together across country. He glanced about him, then said:

"There was no dog. We are all prepared to swear there has never been any dog. Perhaps you would care to hear a short story, *Howaji?* Once on a time there was a very young and a very foolish man. He adopted a stray dog. This was bad enough. But later he boasted loudly that he had named the unclean beast after his sacred majesty, the Sultan—on whom be Peace!

"Today we enter the garrison city of Nablous. There are men among us, perhaps, who would gladly earn money by reporting to the commandant the story I have just told you. If they did, that foolish young foreigner might spend much time in a prison, before his government could hear of him. So also might his dragoman and others of his party. But if there is no dog, and if the best of us are ready to take oath that there has never been any dog, then that foolish young American will be safe. Therefore there is no dog. I have seen to that."

My silly speech had cost the life of a loyal little chum.

A NAMELESS MONGREL
Who Repaid a Kindness

EDMUND SINGER, of Kennetcook Corner, near Halifax, Nova Scotia, fed and sheltered a lost mongrel dog. The dog seemed grateful and hung around his shack for a time. Then he disappeared.

Singer was hurrying home one day a month or so later along an icy by-road. A heavy snowstorm had set in—a storm that was merging into a blizzard. The mercury was far below zero. The man was none too warmly dressed. His foot slipped on a sheet of ice, hidden from sight by the fast falling snow. Down went Singer with a crash, breaking his right leg. There he lay, helpless, unable to move.

Few, if any, would pass along that isolated by-road during such a blizzard. Singer was in immediate danger of freezing to death.

Then it was that a dark figure appeared, apparently from nowhere, through that white welter of snow. It was the nameless mongrel dog Singer had befriended. The dog sniffed eagerly at the fallen and helpless man, then dashed off into the storm.

Joseph Barron, a lumberman, was plodding along a main road, some distance away, when a dog sprang out of the swirl of snow and caught him by the hem of the coat. The dog whimpered and tugged, beside himself with excitement. Barron realized the dog wanted him to come somewhere, and he followed to where Singer lay, half-dead in a drift. The lumberman lifted the swooning sufferer with much difficulty, and helped him to the nearest house.

The mongrel capered ahead, barking in gay triumph—the mongrel who had repaid Singer's kindness by saving him from death.

FLASH
Pointing a Mile-Distant Pheasant

IF THIS yarn had not been verified by the New York newspapers and by the police and by several local residents, I should class it as a "tall story" and forbear to tell it to you.

Flash was a ticked-and-white English setter, lithe and agile in brain as well as in body. She was an inspired field dog; and she had hardly an equal in the art of "pointing" a game bird.

Most of you understand that term "point," as applied to a trained hunting dog. To those of you who don't, I'll explain it in a handful of words.

When a good dog gets the scent—faint or strong—of a game bird, when he is out in the fields or woods with his master, he has a mystic sense which tells him whether the bird is near by or far away.

If it is far away he moves cautiously in the direction of the scent. If it is at all close to him, he "points" it. In other words, he stands as still as a statue, usually with one front paw lifted and with his tail straight out, and with his nose in the precise direction of the bird.

There he will stand, pointing, until his master approaches. At the latter's word, he will either advance a few steps, cautiously, to "flush" the bird (make it fly up) or will remain moveless while his master shoots.

At the shot, a well-trained dog will drop to the ground or remain standing where he is, until he is ordered to go forward to find the shot bird and carry it back to his master. He will carry the game so gently that not a feather will be ruffled. And he will drop it at his master's

Pointing a Mile-Distant Pheasant

feet or slip it into his pocket or game bag. No other canine works so deftly and inspiredly as the rightly trained bird dog. I have known several of them so fanatical in their field tasks that they have refused to go on hunting with a man who has missed two or three shots in succession.

Let's get back to Flash, shan't we?

Flash belonged to George U. Harvey, president of Queens Borough, New York City. Harvey was rightly proud of his setter's prowess as a field dog, and used to boast to his friends: "If there is an English pheasant a mile away, that setter of mine will nose it out and find just where it is."

He had no idea how soon and how literally Flash was going to prove the truth of his boast.

One evening, Harvey had to go to Manhattan Island on business. Flash went everywhere with him when he was in his own borough of Queens, but on this night, Harvey tied her in the cellar of his home, before he went to town.

What happened next, nobody knows. But Flash must have slipped free from her leash and found some means of getting out of the house. Presumably, then, she set forth on a hunting trip, on her own account, though game is less than scarce in that borough.

A little more than a mile away from the Harvey home lived Humbert De Pamphilis, a man who had a queer pet which he loved as much as Harvey loved Flash. This pet was an English pheasant, which De Pamphilis had raised from a chick, and which lived in the house with him and was his constant companion.

For instance, the pheasant always sat in the living-room with its master, during the evenings, listening to the radio. When bedtime

Old Gentleman Joe   Diana Thorne

Pointing a Mile-Distant Pheasant

came, the bird used to follow its owner upstairs to his room, and perch on the foot of his bed for the night. It was as good as an alarm clock, for promptly at six forty-five each morning it waked De Pamphilis by its loud squalling. In brief, it was an honored and privileged member of the family.

One night, after listening to the radio, De Pamphilis went to bed early. As usual, the pheasant followed him to his room and settled down for the night on the foot of the bed.

The man was tired, and he went to sleep at once. He was awakened by a series of loud squalls from the pheasant. Switching on the light, he found it was nowhere near morning. This was the first time the bird had waked him before six forty-five.

Then De Pamphilis noticed that the squalling came from the living-room, downstairs, and that it was accompanied by an irregular and excited tinkling sound. He hurried down to investigate, turning on all the lights as he went.

There in the living-room was the pheasant. It was running up and down the keyboard of the piano. At every excited step, the keys tinkled discordantly under the pressure of the splayed claws. And at every step the pheasant squalled loudly in terror. It was a double din, raucous enough to wake the dead. Evidently the bird was in a state of wild terror.

De Pamphilis glanced around the lighted room to find out what had excited his pet. There, in the doorway leading to the front hall, stood a ticked English setter. The dog was "frozen to a point."

The bird gave a shrill squawk at sight of its master, and flew for refuge to De Pamphilis' shoulder. The dog merely changed its own position enough to level its nose at the pheasant in the latter's new position.

Pointing a Mile-Distant Pheasant

De Pamphilis backed toward a cupboard door, opened the door and thrust the pheasant into the cupboard, and then slammed the door shut after his pet.

The dog proceeded to point the closed door.

De Pamphilis telephoned for the local police. He stuttered out a story so strange and unbelievable that Patrolmen Schatt and Larkin came to his house on the dead run.

Meanwhile, the dog made no effort at all to attack De Pamphilis, but continued to stand, steady as a rock, pointing that cupboard door.

De Pamphilis made the rounds of the house, to find how the setter had gotten in. That is a part of the general mystery. Every door and every window was shut and locked—or so De Pamphilis declared to the police as they came hurrying to the scene. (To this day, nobody knows how the setter got into the house.)

Both the patrolmen recognized the intruder as Flash, the beloved bird dog of their borough president. They knew how carefully Harvey always shut up the setter when he was away from home. And that added to the mystery.

They led Flash to the police station and telephoned Harvey to come and get her, which he did.

That's all the story. But it proved Harvey's boast that Flash could find a pheasant "a mile away."

WOTAN
The Police Dog Who Fought a Leopard

THIS yarn would make a gorgeous motion picture of the Rin-Tin-Tin sort. Several African newspapers—from Johannesburg and elsewhere—telling the story in vivid detail, were sent to me. I have every reason to believe it is true.

Mr. Sandys, a missionary, was assigned to the Buta district in the Belgian Congo. He took out with him his two big German police dogs, Wotan and Juno. In that wild region a house dog is not a mere pet for a foreign resident. There are marauding wild beasts. There are none-too-friendly natives.

Almost directly after their arrival, the two police dogs taught native thieves that the Sandys bungalow was an exceedingly good place to keep away from. Skulking wild animals, too, learned to give the mission a wide berth.

The bungalow was small. In one of its wings was the missionary's bedroom. In a storage room just off of this slept the police dogs. From this room a door led out onto the veranda. It swung both ways. Thus the dogs could charge out through it, in response to any alarm, and could return again to their sleeping mats, merely by pushing against the light portal.

Once or twice in the nights, they heard stealthy steps in the garden outside and dashed forth to repel the intruders. In each case these intruders proved to be supposedly harmless villagers prowling around the bungalow grounds from idle curiosity. At least that was their story. But the dogs had not waited to find out if the midnight visitors were harm-

The Police Dog Who Fought a Leopard

less or not. They had rushed at them and pulled them down and were industriously chewing them when the missionary rescued the howling victims.

That kind of thing did not tend to make the dogs popular. There were threats of poison; there were remonstrances from the local authorities. So Mr. Sandys sent to the nearest city for two stout muzzles which he always strapped on the dogs' noses at night. Thus Wotan and Juno would still be able to fly out at marauders but could do them no actual harm beyond upsetting them. To make certain of his own safety, now that his guards were rendered useless in case of night attacks, Sandys loaded his double-barreled gun with buckshot cartridges and hung it just above the swinging door, where he could grab it on his way out.

A few months later Juno presented her mate with a litter of six healthy little police dog pups. Sandys rigged up a broodnest for her in a corner of the outer room where she and Wotan slept. There Juno used to spend her nights, with her six babies cuddled close to her, while Wotan stretched himself out near the swinging door, on guard over his mate and his babies as well as his master.

One red-hot night a leopard chanced to be roving not far from the mission. To his keen nostrils came the scent of the puppies. Now, for some reason, a leopard would rather dine on dogs than on any other fare, and puppies are the most irresistibly toothsome food he can find. The roving leopard crept up to the bungalow and encircled it without a sound. Presently he came to the swinging door. Here the scent was much stronger. He abandoned all caution, and hurled himself at the door. It swung inward under his impact and he was in the room.

Then it was that Wotan went into sudden action. Probably the big dog had heard or scented the leopard as the beast prowled

The Police Dog Who Fought a Leopard

around the house. But undoubtedly Wotan had realized how helpless he was with his own jaws strapped, so had stayed where he was.

But when the leopard actually burst into the room, it became a matter of stark need to defend Juno and their six pups. So, handicapped as he was, Wotan sprang upon the leopard. The leopard grappled him, while Juno filled the night with her barking. The barking, the growling, the thumping of the two battling brutes on the floor—these filled the bungalow with a most unearthly din.

Sandys awoke and came running to the scene, stopping only to light his bedroom lamp, which showed him the fighters tangled in a death grip. And they were between him and his gun!

The missionary crept cautiously around the combatants with what speed he could. As he reached the gun and snatched it from its hook, he saw the leopard sink his teeth deep into valiant Wotan's back.

Then Sandys fired both barrels into the spotted monster.

One of the pellets ricocheted from the floor and broke the lamp, putting it out. Sandys was in total darkness, in the room with a leopard which his volley might or might not have hit. The din of battle ceased. The only sounds in the black room were the woebegone moaning of Juno and the soft squealing of her suddenly awakened puppies.

Sandys found a matchbox and struck a light. There in the middle of the room, surrounded by a tumble of broken furniture, lay the leopard stone dead. Across his body sprawled Wotan, his back broken by that murderous bite which Sandys had seen.

Wotan died two days later, but I think few animals have perished more gallantly than did this grand police dog that went, muzzled, into hopeless death battle to save his mate and babies.

ROGER
The Church-Going Bloodhound

ROGER was a bloodhound. He belonged to Rev. Morton Leslie who was the Episcopal rector in a suburb of Liverpool, England, almost ninety years ago. Perhaps because his master was a clergyman—or for some more special reason—Roger developed a craze for going to church. As he was the rector's dog and as he always lay quietly at the foot of the pulpit stairs, nobody complained.

Always the bloodhound would pace solemnly to church with his master for every Sunday or week-day service. Always he would march up the aisle and would stretch himself on the floor in his chosen place just beneath the pulpit. Always he lay there without sound or motion until the service was at an end.

What pleasure this lively dog found in lying so still for an hour or more at a time—and three times a day on Sundays—nobody could guess. But Roger allowed nothing to keep him away, and in the course of time the congregation became so used to his presence at the foot of the pulpit that they did not even notice him.

But one Sunday morning he was brought to their attention in a most startling fashion.

Mr. Leslie had a bad sore throat, which made it impossible for him to speak above a whisper, though he was well enough to go to church. So he arranged for a fellow-clergyman to take that day's services.

As usual, Roger strode up the aisle and curled himself to rest in his regular place below the pulpit. It did not seem to strike him as strange that his master was sitting in one of the pews instead of of-

Big Boy Diana Thorne

The Tail of Hoffman Diana Thorne

The Church-Going Bloodhound

ficiating at the altar. Then the substitute clergyman came out of the vestry, and advanced toward the rail. *Toward* the rail; not *to* the rail. He never got that far.

With a wild beast roar, the bloodhound leaped up and rushed murderously at the newcomer who was usurping his dear master's official duties. He flung himself upon the substitute preacher, bore him to the floor and was ravening at his throat. The church was in an uproar. The scandalized worshipers screamed or shouted or mounted the pew-seats to get out of the supposedly rabid bloodhound's way. One or two people threw hymn books and pew cushions at him.

Meanwhile, Mr. Leslie had kept his head. Being speechless from his sore throat, he could not call to Roger to desist from attacking the newcomer. But he could, and did, run foward at top speed and drag the raging bloodhound away from his victim.

A member of the family led Roger home in black disgrace. The substitute was induced to go on with the service. The congregation settled down and tried to forget the shock to their collective nerves. The incident seemed to be ended. It was not.

Never thereafter did Roger make the slightest effort to accompany his clerical master to church. Never willingly would he set foot on the church street. In fact, every Sunday morning just before church-time, he sneaked out of the house and wandered away, not returning until the Leslie family got back home for lunch. He seemed to understand he had done a horrible thing in breaking up the service and mauling the stranger.

The Leslies were sorry for him. They supposed the dog was cured forever of the church habit. Then something happened which showed how mistaken they were.

About a month later, a Mrs. Harris accosted Mr. Leslie in the street

The Church-Going Bloodhound

and demanded furiously to know what he meant by insulting her religion.

The clergyman gaped at her in astonishment. He had met the woman only once or twice. But he knew her to be a zealous member of another religious denomination, a denomination which worshiped in a chapel at the opposite end of the suburb. For some reason there had been a feud of long standing between many persons in the chapel's congregation and part of the membership of Mr. Leslie's church.

Both pastors had tried to bring about a better understanding, but just when their peaceful efforts seemed to be succeeding, something evidently had happened to stir up fresh trouble between the congregations. Therefore, Mr. Leslie was keenly worried at the hostile tone of Mrs. Harris.

He assured her he had done nothing to warrant such a scolding, and he begged her to explain what she meant. Mrs. Harris was only too eager to explain. She declared hotly:

"You trained that great hulking bloodhound of yours to come to our chapel every Sunday morning, just at the beginning of service, and to go to the bottom of the pulpit and lie down there. You did it to make fun of us and to spoil our services. You knew we wouldn't dare lay hands on such a dangerous brute and put him out of the church. But we are going to law about it."

In vain did Mr. Leslie try to make her understand that he had not trained Roger to do anything of the kind and that he had not even known of his dog's Sunday visits to the chapel. Then the perplexed rector went to call on the other minister. He found that Mrs. Harris' tale was true.

Every Sunday, since the time Roger had attacked the clergyman who was officiating in his master's church, the dog had traveled all the

The Church-Going Bloodhound

way to the chapel and had lain at the foot of the pulpit throughout the morning service.

Although both ministers tried to make the malcontents realize that Mr. Leslie could not possibly have taught his dog such a trick, the more embittered members of the chapel congregation continued to believe it was by Mr. Leslie's orders.

None of the extracts from the papers tell how the tale ended—whether or not the church-and-chapel feud was patched up, and whether or not Roger was cured permanently of his mania for attending places of divine worship.

I wish I knew.

GRIP
The Eighteenth Century Canine Thief

EARLY in the eighteenth century, London and its suburbs were teeming with crooks of every kind, from masked highwaymen to petty food-snatchers. One of the craftiest thieves of the time was Tom Gerrard, who seems to have used his brains to better effect than did most of his fellow-blackguards. His cleverest and safest way of robbing was through the help of his beautiful mongrel dog, Grip.

Tom Gerrard had a genius for dog-training. Grip had a genius for learning. It was a good combination, except for its many victims. The dog had a keen scent, and was easily taught to detect the odor of leather. With that leather-smelling background to work from, Gerrard would hide in a doorway of an alley which opened on a busy London street. At his command, Grip would trot out into the street and mingle with the passers-by. The rest of his training was easily acquired.

I have said the dog was handsome. Also he had a most winning and lovable personality. He was the kind of dog which strangers instinctively speak to or stoop down to pat. That was his chief asset for the trade which Gerrard had taught him.

Grip would single out some well-dressed man among the pedestrians and would run up to him playfully, dancing about him and trying in his winsome fashion to make friends. Few could resist pausing to pet such a dog. As the stranger bent down to stroke him, Grip's scenting powers would be busy locating the leather wallet or pocketbook his new friend was carrying. He would make a sudden dive at the pocket which contained it.

The Eighteenth Century Canine Thief

With one skilled wrench of his powerful jaws, he would rip loose the pocket and the pocketbook it contained, and would dash off down the street at top speed, carrying his plunder between his teeth. Naturally, the despoiled man would think it was only a bit of destructive playfulness, and he would give chase.

But never did he get back his stolen wallet. Grip was not only fleet of foot, but he was an inspired dodger. He would plunge into the first convenient alleyway and thence into another, and along some twisting street, and in through the front door of a shop, and out at the back. He knew the whole neighborhood, every inch of it, and it was an absurdly easy matter for him to shake off the most vehement pursuit. No human could possibly hope to catch up with him or to find whither he had gone.

Then, when the chase had died down, Grip would make his way to the alley where Tom Gerrard was hiding, and would push the pocketbook into his master's hand. Gerrard would empty out the money and throw away the wallet. After which, the same trick would be performed again at some spot a mile or more distant.

It was a lucrative mode of making a living. Gerrard himself ran no risk at all. Grip was in little more danger than was his master, for his skill and his speed safeguarded him from capture. Perhaps Gerrard might have continued to live comfortably for years on his dog's thefts if he had been satisfied with such modest earnings. But he heard of the big sums won by highwaymen on Hampstead Heath and elsewhere, and he yearned to become rich in the same way. So he set up as a highwayman and was captured almost at once. He was tried and found guilty. In August of 1711 he was hanged.

Poor masterless Grip mourned bitterly for his master. There was nobody left to take care of him, nobody left to steal for.

The Eighteenth Century Canine Thief

As he wandered disconsolately around the streets, he attracted the notice of Dr. Burgess, a Presbyterian clergyman. The kind-hearted minister took Grip home with him. The dog eagerly accepted Dr. Burgess as his master, and grew devoted to him.

One day the clergyman went into a shop to make several purchases. He left Grip on the threshold. When Dr. Burgess came out, his new dog had vanished and, believing Grip had been stolen or had strayed of his own will, the minister went sadly home. But just before he reached his own door, the dog overtook him. With tail wagging and eyes alight with joy, Grip thrust a leathern purse into the clergyman's hand.

Dr. Burgess opened the purse and found it contained a small handful of silver and of coppers, but no means of identifying the loser. He supposed it had fallen from someone's pocket, and that Grip had found it lying in the street and had brought it home. He made inquiries in the neighborhood, but nobody claimed the treasure trove. So Dr. Burgess put the money into his church's Poor Fund, and thought no more about the trivial matter.

But two days later it was brought sharply to his attention again. He paid a pastoral visit to one of his parishioners. Grip went along. Dr. Burgess told him to wait on the doorstep. It was a long visit. When the clergyman came out of the house, Grip stood on the step, eagerly welcoming him as before, and thrust into his hand a fat leather wallet.

Dr. Burgess was dumfounded. While it was quite possible that his dog should have found one purse lying lost on the pavement, it was beyond all probability that he should have found two lost purses in two days. The cash went into the Poor Fund, and Dr. Burgess told the queer story to several people.

These people presumably told it to others, for presently Grip was

The Eighteenth Century Canine Thief

identified as the dog that had been stealing leather pocketbooks and purses for years. Also someone identified him as Tom Gerrard's dog. Through a "squealing" crook, the police had at last learned of the trick which Gerrard had taught his dog. The case was complete. Grip had gone on playing his old game for the benefit of his new master.

Dr. Burgess felt it was too risky and too dishonest to keep on owning a dog of such lawless talents. He decided to cure Grip of the purse-stealing habit in the only way he believed such a dog could be cured. He hanged the dog in his garden, even as Grip's master had been hanged on Tyburn Hill. Dogs in England, for centuries, had been put to death by hanging, so perhaps Dr. Burgess' punishment of Grip was less barbarous than it would seem nowadays. Nevertheless the poor mongrel had not consciously done anything to merit death. He had only been trying to make a hit with his new owner.

HALIL
The Saluki Hero of a Strange Contest

SOME of you have seen the Saluki—the Afghan hound—at dog shows and elsewhere during the past few years. There are only a few of them in America thus far, though they are becoming popular in Europe, and though they have been used for hunting in various parts of the Orient for centuries. The dogs are of various colors, and they look like rather small greyhounds with shaggy tails, and with longer hair than the greyhound's. They are incredibly swift runners. Their Oriental masters use them chiefly for hunting antelopes.

The hero of this story was a Saluki named Halil, the Arabic word for *The Well-Loved.* He lived up to his name, for he was the favorite possession of Uthman, lord of the Kifri tribe. Uthman loved the beautiful brown-and-silver hound, and kept Halil at his side, wherever his tribe wandered. The dog slept at his master's feet at night in the royal tent, and ate all his meals with him. This in a land where a dog usually is regarded as unclean.

But Halil deserved his master's favor. He was an inspired hunter and faster in the chase than any other dog in that region. Fleet indeed must be the desert antelope which Halil could not run to earth.

To westward of the Kifri domains lay the country of Beni Zor, of which Ysouf was chief. He was Uthman's mortal foe. Time and again the two tribes had clashed. In fair battle the Kifri warriors nearly always were victorious, but in craftiness—such as the successful raiding of unprotected Kifri flocks and herds and supplies of grain—Ysouf's men were far more successful.

"Rats!" Diana Thorne

Salukis Diana Thorne

The Saluki Hero of a Strange Contest

It was a hereditary feud. Then, because each side was exhausted and becoming impoverished, a truce was patched up between them. Uthman and Ysouf were as bitter enemies as ever, but it was good policy just then to hide this mutual hatred and to pretend to be friends. As part of this friendly policy, a grand hunt was arranged.

Now one of Uthman's fiercest grievances against Ysouf was that the chief of the Beni Zor owned a big jet black Saluki, Shaitan by name (Arabic for *Devil*), which Ysouf had always declared was twice as fleet and three times as brave and clever as the gentle Halil.

Ysouf had joked unkindly about Halil and about Uthman's devotion to his dog, and had said Shaitan could race the legs off the Kifri dog. So, craftily, Ysouf now proposed that the hunt begin with a race between the two mighty hounds.

Eagerly, Uthman accepted the challenge. He saw a chance to humiliate his lifelong foe in the presence of all their tribesmen by the defeat of the black dog of which the Beni Zor men bragged so loudly.

These were to be the conditions of the contest: the two chiefs and their respective dogs were to go out to a gully which was a favorite feeding place for antelopes. The hounds were to be held in leash until one of the "beaters" should scare up an antelope and send it scudding away, over the flat miles of sands just beyond. Then, at a signal, Halil and Shaitan were to be let loose. Whichever of them should first overtake the antelope, and pull it down, was to be adjudged winner of the race. The test would prove, once and for all, which of the hounds was the faster.

The morning of the hunt arrived. The two chiefs, each holding his dog by the leash, stationed themselves upon a hillock. Behind them the sands were black with spectators. Beaters crept forward to the

The Saluki Hero of a Strange Contest

gully. Presently an antelope flashed up the slope in terrified flight and across the desert.

The signal was given. Uthman and Ysouf unleashed their straining dogs. Both hounds had caught sight of the antelope. Both tore away at top speed in pursuit of their prey. The race was on!

The chiefs and their retinues sprang to the backs of their horses and galloped after the fast-flying dogs. Arab-like, they scourged their steeds to a mad run, while the riders spun their long muskets high in the air and screeched encouragement to the hounds.

Across the sands sped the antelope. Closer and closer to the fugitive raced the two Salukis, neck and neck, and behind them thundered the chiefs and their followers.

For a time the two hounds had been running side by side, without an inch of advantage. Now, slowly but steadily, Halil was forging ahead. The pace was too hot for the black hound. Halil was winning. Everyone could see that.

Ysouf swung his inlaid musket high in air. As the weapon came down, he leveled it as if by accident at the brown-and-silver Saluki, and pulled trigger. He had staked a fortune on that race. Now he saw himself about to lose, and he took the only method of saving his bets. Moreover, he knew how bitterly unhappy Uthman would be at the loss of his loved dog. It would be easy to swear it had been an accident, and to offer profuse apologies.

Just as Ysouf fired, Shaitan swerved to the right, directly between his master and Halil. The bullet imbedded itself deeply in the black dog's body. With a yelp of agony, Shaitan rolled over, dead.

WOLF
Our Great Little Collie

WOLF was the son of Lad, whose adventures some of you have read. As a puppy, he was one of the most unpromising specimens I have raised. He was wildly mischievous and lawless, and he had not a single physical trait of the true show-type of collie. He was uncannily clever, though, and fearless, and he looked like a young timber wolf, except that his coat was fierily red.

His temper was as fiery as his coat. However, to the Mistress and myself he was gentleness itself. We could do anything with him. My roughest romping never evoked so much as a growl or a snap. He would not even bite us in play, as do most romping dogs. He seemed to know a bite is an effort to kill, and not to be used in romping.

To the rest of the world—except to trespassers and tramps and the like—he was severely standoffish, so long as the rest of the world consented to adopt the same attitude toward him. But he would not allow anyone else to lay the tip of a finger on him.

If an outsider sought to pet him or so much as touch him, Wolf resented it silently and fiercely, by a leap for the throat. We used to warn guests at Sunnybank to leave him severely alone, and we promised that Wolf would return the courtesy by not molesting them in any way. He kept to his share of the bargain.

It was he who rode always in the car with us. At first he and Bruce, then he and my big collie-chum, Bobby. Wolf guarded that car with fierce zeal. Let anyone lay a hand on it while Wolf was aboard, or so much as brush against it in passing, and Wolf was at him.

Our Great Little Collie

There was only one exception to this. One evening as we waited at the Pompton Lakes post office for our mail, a friend came up and began to talk to us. His voice was not quite steady as he told us how his own loved collie had been killed that day by a motor car. As the man talked he laid his arm on the car seat.

Wolf lurched past us toward him. But instead of growling, or biting him, the collie leaned out and licked the man's unhappy face. It was the first and last time I ever saw him caress anyone but ourselves. The man even petted the sympathetic dog, and Wolf endured it patiently and gently.

Six months later we met the same man again, outside the post office. As he laid his hand on the car door, Wolf flew ragingly at him.

When Wolf was about a year old there were several tiny collie puppies playing on the driveway that leads down through the woods from the main road to our house. A car came rapidly down the drive, toward the pups. Instantly Wolf rounded them up, as cleverly as the best-trained collie could round up an unruly bunch of sheep. He herded them out of the path of the approaching car and to safety.

The Mistress praised him highly for this wise bit of ancestral instinct. That was enough. Wolf saw he had made a hit. From then on, he used to delight in herding to safety every animal, from puppies to cows, that chanced to get on the driveway. And always he would come galloping to us for praise and petting.

I wish now that we had discouraged him from the start, and had broken him of the trick. For if we had, he might still be alive. But it became a habit of his to clear the drive of anything and everything as soon as a car came in sight. He did it deftly and snappily.

As he grew older, he became somewhat gentler to accredited friends

Our Great Little Collie

of ours. Not that he encouraged them to be familiar with him. But no longer did he snap at them when they tried to pet him.

To my mother he constituted himself a volunteer protector. Once as she and I were walking, an Airedale passed us in the road. My mother's cloak-hem chanced to brush the Airedale along the side. He snarled at her. Instantly, Wolf hurled himself upon him and gave him the most spectacular beating I ever saw administered.

When we got home we told the Mistress about this, and she praised him. Immediately, Wolf trotted off to the Airedale's house, a mile distant, and thrashed him all over again. That was always his way. Let the Mistress praise him for anything and instantly he proceeded to do it once more, to win more praise.

One afternoon, when he was about ten years old, a big delivery truck came spinning down the drive. Bobby was asleep there. Wolf swooped upon him, tugging and shoving him out of the way of the advancing truck. He got Bobby clear of the danger, but the truck fender grazed his own shoulder. I said then, for the tenth time, that some day a car would strike and kill him, swift and wise though he was.

On the same evening, the Mistress and myself were away for dinner. Wolf went for an evening stroll. His walk led him across the railroad tracks. He had a wholesome respect for trains ever since seeing a puppy cut in two by one. As ever, he looked up and down the track to see if the way was clear. Some people on the steps of trackside cottages were watching him. Barely had Wolf gotten safely across when a mongrel cur came loping along. The cur sat down in the middle of the track and began to scratch a flea. At the same moment the express train, from around the bend, sounded its whistle. Wolf glanced back and saw the mongrel still sitting there, scratching.

Our Great Little Collie

Around the curve tore the express. The mongrel crouched in terror at the blaze of its headlight. Then Wolf did what he had been in training all his life to do. He sprang back onto the track, seized the cur by the nape of its neck and hurled it down into the trackside ditch, to safety. Then he himself, in the same motion, leaped from the rails.

Almost he was in time. But an outjutting bit of metal touched the side of his head, as he was in mid-air. He was dead before he struck ground.

Perhaps there are less heroic things than "dying like a dog."

VIGI
The Hero Dog of the Vikings

KING OLAF had reconquered the kingdom of Norway, which had been snatched from his father. Having conquered it, he proceeded to convert it from heathenism and from the worship of the old Norse gods, Odin and Thor and the other Scandinavian deities.

The king hit on a very simple and very effective way of converting these heathen. He offered them their choice between baptism and death. After he had shown, by a few terrible examples, that he was in earnest, conversions became popular, even wholesale, throughout Norway.

Having converted his own kingdom, Olaf set out to do some active missionary work elsewhere. His procedure was as simple as it had been in Norway and it was far more profitable. He would swoop down with his war-galleys and his horde of savage Vikings on some weaker country, and would conquer and pillage it. Then he would offer its subdued inhabitants their choice between the Gospel and the Sword.

Their choice was almost unanimous. Land after land became converted. Olaf grew richer and richer. To do him justice, there can be little doubt he was sincere in his religious faith and in his methods of converting others. It was an iron age, and he and his country were just emerging from barbarism.

Down swooped the war-galleys of Norway upon Ireland. The throng of shield-hung ships were bristling with shaggy men-at-arms. Giant slaves tugged at the oars, while whip-brandishing officers walked up and down the lines of rowers, flogging them to their task. Far ahead of the rest of the Viking fleet sailed the *Long Serpent*, Olaf's flagship.

The Hero Dog of the Vikings

The Vikings landed and began their invasion of the surrounding country, smashing all opposition, burning farms and villages and seizing everything of value. By the time they turned back toward their ships they were laden with the plunder of Ireland. They drove before them thousands of captured cattle and sheep.

As King Olaf watched the flocks of cattle billowing past him, a rough Irish hill farmer came up to the king and demanded fearlessly:

"Give me back my cattle, oh Norseman! Surely my small flock of twenty will not be missed by you, out of the many thousand you have seized. Yet they are my livelihood. I pray you to let me take them."

The king laughed aloud at such effrontery. Yet he was pleased by the Irishman's courage in making the request. Olaf loved a joke. So he said: "Your plea is granted. Yonder are thousands and thousands of cattle, all mingled together in one vast drove. Pick your twenty out of that turmoil and you shall have them. But be sure to pick only your own twenty, and none others."

The Irishman was not discouraged at the seemingly impossible task. He whistled long and shrilly. In answer to his summons, a huge hound came galloping down from the wooded hill behind him. At a gesture from his master, the dog rushed into the milling myriads of cattle.

Swiftly, unerringly, the hound picked out one after another of his own master's cattle, driving each of them free from the herd, until all twenty were bunched safely by themselves on the hillside. Then the hound looked to the Irishman for further orders.

King Olaf was delighted at the exhibition of cleverness. He declared the great dog must be his. As he had stolen forcibly everything else he could lay hands on in Ireland, it would have been logical for him to

The Hero Dog of the Vikings

steal the hound, too. But the Irishman's pluck and resource had won his admiration. Drawing from his own arm the heavy golden bracelet he wore, he gave it to the man in exchange for the dog.

From that hour the hound was Olaf's chosen comrade. He named him Vigi, and took him everywhere with him. Vigi learned to love the king as he had once loved and served his Irish master. He lay at Olaf's side during the wild wassail feasts that celebrated each victory. He slept at the foot of the king's couch. He voyaged with his royal master on Olaf's various warlike expeditions, and he fought at the king's side during the shore raids. The giant dog and the ferocious sea-king were inseparable. The rough Vikings adopted Vigi as a chum, too.

Then Raud the Strong, and others who hated the king and who refused conversion, made their headquarters on an island off the Norway coast, defying Olaf to dislodge them from their sea-girt stronghold. Olaf and his Viking fleet sailed down on them with Vigi, as ever, close to the king.

The Vikings fought their way ashore, amid a whirlwind of arrows and flung spears. Leading them and far in advance of his men charged Olaf, the king. At his side raged Vigi. The leader of the rebels turned and fled, as the king rushed at him with the savage dog for comrade-at-arms.

Vigi flashed ahead of his royal master and seized the rebel chief before the fugitive had fled ten steps. The rebel wheeled about and drove his spear through the gallant dog, just as Olaf caught up with him.

At a blow, Olaf struck the chief dead.

The Vikings were making short work of the island's other defenders. Presently all the rebels were slain or captured. Back trooped the cheering Vikings with Sigurd and young Tamberskelvar leading them. Back

The Hero Dog of the Vikings

to receive the praise of their king. But Olaf had no thought for anything except the hero dog, lying there at his feet.

He bade the Vikings lift Vigi on a shield and bear him back to the ship with royal honors, as they would have carried a slain or wounded prince. Then he himself set to work dressing the spear-wound in the hound's great body.

Day and night Olaf worked over Vigi, until at last the dog was well again.

Katherine Lee Bates has written a stirring poem from the true tale. Its last stanza runs:

> "Now proud of heart was Vigi to be borne to ship on shield,
> And for many a day thereafter, when the bitter thrust had healed,
> The dog would leap on the Vikings and coax with his Irish wit
> Till 'mid laughter a shield was leveled—and Vigi rode on it!"

MAFEKING
A War Dog of South Africa

THIRTY-ODD years ago Mafeking's name was as well known to English troops in South Africa as were the names of their generals. He was a shaggy and ragged Irish terrier, named from the Boer town which was the crucial strategic point of so much of that war.

Nobody seems to recall where the terrier came from nor how he chanced to attach himself to one of the British regiments that defended the besieged city. But instantly he won for himself a welcome among the troops, and he became a self-appointed mascot to his regiment. He was a venturesome chap, like nearly all Irish terriers. Instead of staying safely behind walls and houses, he insisted on getting out into the open, and under direct range of the Boer marksmen's fire, but the Boers were endowed with too much sportsmanship to kill dogs.

Time after time, Mafeking wandered around in the direct line of fire, and not a shot was aimed at him. Then one day, refusing to consider himself besieged, he strolled into the front line defenses which just then happened to be under particularly galling fire from the gunners of the Staats Artillery.

One or two soldiers ordered Mafeking to go back, but he kept on. He was an Irish terrier and a fearless fighter and he was not minded to skulk behind the bombproofs while a battle was going on. So he eluded the several hands which sought to grab him and to thrust him back from harm's way. On he trotted to the outermost defenses. Then he scrambled over a parapet and out into the open, moving unconcernedly, straight toward the Boer batteries.

A War Dog of South Africa

Now here is a bit of clean sportsmanship on the part of the Boer gunners which it is a pleasure to record:

The moment the shaggy little auburn dog came in sight, in the direct line of fire, the Boer batteries fell silent. Not a shell was hurled at the trenches in front of which the gallant terrier was strutting as if he realized the stir which his presence on the firing line was causing. Not a shot was fired until he wearied of his stroll and obeyed the frantic shouts of the soldiers calling him back behind the shelter of the parapet.

Perhaps this was the only time in the history of warfare when whole batteries ceased firing in order to save a dog from death.

Then one day, when he was wandering around in the comparative safety of a street far back in the city, Mafeking was struck by a fragment of shell and was badly hurt. It was a chance shot, and it found the very mark which the Boer gunners so kindly had avoided a few days earlier.

The little dog's wound caused as much concern and anxiety among the city's defenders as if a general officer had been hit. The best medical and surgical care were his during his illness. Disdaining to whine, even when the pain was sharpest, Mafeking bore his injury with gay fortitude. The moment he was able to get on his feet again, he was trying to make his way out into the open and into the zone of artillery fire.

So far from profiting by his painful lesson in caution, the terrier seemed to feel he could not possibly be hit again, or he did not care if he was. But by strict vigilance he was kept out of danger and not allowed to risk his life.

The Irish dog repaid well the care squandered on him. One night, for example, he was asleep in a barrack dormitory, supposedly out of danger from bombardment. At midnight he woke, and began rushing

A War Dog of South Africa

about from room to room, making a most frightful din and tugging at the sleepers' blankets.

The whole dormitory was aroused by his racket. As soon as this was accomplished, Mafeking rushed to the outer doors, then back, and then out again, very evidently urging his human friends to join him outside. So eager was he that the soldiers good-naturedly followed him out, curious as to the cause of his frenzied excitement.

There were only a comparatively few men quartered in that one detached dormitory, but those few owed their lives to Mafeking. For even as they followed him out into the courtyard, a shell hit the building, demolishing it.

During the ensuing bombardment, poor little Mafeking was wounded a second time, as he was trotting across the Market Square. This time he could not get the appetizing titbits that were fed to him during his former illness, for the city was half starved, and the chief diet was horseflesh gravy and husks and oats mixed with a sweetish decoction of glycerine. Nevertheless, Mafeking got well. He did more. After the siege was lifted, he accompanied his regiment through the rest of the campaign, and then returned to England in triumph with it at the end of the war.

WALLACE
Glasgow's Immortal Fire Dog

HE LOOKED like a red-brown collie, shaggy and alert. But then he looked more or less like several other kinds of dog. His breed doesn't matter. If he was of mongrel blood, he was also of uncannily clever brain and of hero heart.

His name was Wallace. At least, that was the name he bore with honor during much of his life. Nobody knows where he came from nor who first owned him. His history begins on a hot day in 1896, when he strolled into the Central Fire Hall, on College Street in Glasgow, Scotland, and lay down under the nearest engine.

He did not slink into the place, but behaved as if he belonged there and as if the cool floor under the engine were his regular bed. He had the air of a dog that has come home.

But the firemen could not see it that way. The dog was hauled out from beneath the engine, by the scruff of the neck, and was kicked into the street. In less than a minute he was back again. With a reproachful glance at the fireman who had ejected him, he curled up once more under his chosen engine. That was all the good it did him. For another fireman hit him over the head and kicked him once more into the roadway. And, once more, he was back beneath the engine in less than no time. After this performance of eviction and return had been repeated five times, the firemen got tired of such violent exercise on such a hot day, and they let the dog lie undisturbed.

A few minutes later came an alarm of fire. It was a dangerous blaze. The engines dashed out in response to the call. On the first of

Glasgow's Immortal Fire Dog

them rode Chief Patterson, the head and the idol of the Glasgow fire fighters. Patterson noticed a red-brown dog galloping directly in front of his engine's horses (it was before the day of motor fire engines) and trying to clear the way for the team. The dog barked at the top of his lungs, and kept rushing at such bystanders as did not get out of the way of the engines as fast as he thought they should.

After the fire was put out and the engines started back for the hall, the same dog led the procession, and once more made valiant efforts to clear the way for it. Chief Patterson was amused at the odd sight. He made inquiries.

Then he decreed that the dog should be allowed to remain as a guest of the Department and to sleep under the Number One Engine which he had chosen as his bed. By a vote of the firemen, the newcomer was named Wallace, in honor of Scotland's national hero. That was the beginning of Wallace's long career as a fire dog.

Patterson had noted that in leading the engines and trucks home from the conflagration, the dog had not once looked back, and yet had gone directly to the fire hall. Presently, another and more notable thing was observed about Wallace. By some queer instinct he seemed to know just where every fire was. The moment the alarm sounded, night or day, the dog was on his feet, and was galloping ahead of the engines and trucks, straight toward the scene of the blaze.

This odd twist of intelligence on his part has never been explained, so far as I can find out. For he did not wait to see which direction the engines would take. Always, he led them where they should go. The firemen grew to regard him with something like awe because of this odd trait of his. They treated him with affection and almost with deference, and they sang his praises everywhere.

Glasgow's Immortal Fire Dog

Soon word of Wallace's peculiar cleverness reached the newspapers. Reporters came to watch him, and to note his behavior when fire alarms were turned in. His praises were sounded in one paper after another throughout Great Britain. He was a national figure.

He was civil to his many visitors and to the horde of curious folk who tried to make friends with him at fires. But always he stood on his dignity with everyone who was not a fireman. He seemed to recognize his fellow-workers as the only people with whom a self-respecting fire dog could decently make friends.

He acknowledged no one man as his master, nor would he accept any fire fighter's house as his home. He belonged under his own engine, and there he stayed between alarms.

It was not long before he proved to the Department and to all Glasgow that he was earning his keep. Many a time in those days, engines and trucks were held up on the way to a conflagration by dense flocks of sheep which jammed the narrow streets from side to side on their journey to the various market-places. Wallace solved this problem with ease. Running far in front of the foremost engine, he would charge into these milling and bleating flocks. In a moment or so he would clear a path amid their crowded ranks, wide enough for his beloved engine drivers to gallop through without incurring damage suits for killed sheep. Many a destructive fire did he enable the engines to put out by this saving of the old-time delays. No longer were the close-packed throngs of sheep a menace.

Once, as the engines were rushing to a fire at full speed, a blind man was crossing a street directly in front of them. In his confusion, the man had started across from the curb at precisely the wrong moment. Wallace whizzed forward, grabbing the blind man by the coat-tails and

Glasgow's Immortal Fire Dog

dragging him by main force back to the sidewalk. This before any of the horrified bystanders could come to the victim's rescue. The dog pulled him to safety, almost from under the very hoofs of the galloping fire horses.

The panic-smitten blind man thought he was attacked by a savage dog. As they reached the curb he beat Wallace cruelly over the head and body with the heavy stick he carried.

If the blows had been struck by any ordinary person, the dog would have been at his throat in an instant. But he seemed to understand that this man was helpless and stricken. He did not resent the beating, but scampered back to his place at the head of the engines.

For this heroic deed, a gold medal was awarded to him by the Royal Humane Society—one of the several hero medals earned by Wallace in his years as a fire dog.

When the dog's feet grew tender from much galloping over hard pavements, a Glasgow shoemaker fitted him for a full set of soft boots. These he wore with great pride for the rest of his long life.

BOBBIE
The Three-Thousand-Mile Collie

EARLY in 1921, when Bobbie was only six weeks old, Mr. Brazier, an Oregon farmer, bought him. In learning to drive cattle on his new master's farm, the puppy was kicked badly by a horse, receiving a scar which he would bear for life. Besides, a small tractor ran over him, injuring one of his hips. By these and other marks, long afterward he was identified along a route of three thousand miles.

Brazier sold his farm a year or so after he bought Bobbie, and sold the dog along with it. The family moved into Silverton, some miles away. But Bobbie had been sold without his own consent. He found his way to Silverton and to his old master's home. This he did so often that at last Brazier bought him back again.

In the late summer of 1923, the Brazier family made a motor tour of the Middle West. Bobbie was taken along. At Wolcott, Indiana, while Bobbie was wandering around the town, the family started away, failing to find him. They drove south into Mexico and after that along the Pacific coast, up through California to Silverton, Oregon, again.

Meanwhile Bobbie had gotten mixed up in a dog fight that carried him far from the garage where his master had lost him. The advertisements, paid for by Brazier, failed to locate the missing dog. Thus, it was up to Bobbie to find his human friends and his old home, unaided. Without help, without other guiding than that of his miraculous "collie sixth sense," he set forth on his seemingly hopeless journey.

For something like three thousand miles he trotted. Through big cities and villages padded his tireless feet; across hot desert sands where

Caught or Found?   Diana Thorne

Junior League Committee   Diana Thorne

The Three-Thousand-Mile Collie

rattlesnakes and wolves menaced him. He swam wide rivers; he circled lakes and waded swamps. He climbed the Rocky Mountains, sometimes by trails, sometimes by trackless crag routes where a misstep meant death and where catamounts and bears and the wolf-pack were in wait for lone canines.

Through the sickening desert heat of summer and the blizzards of the Rocky Mountain winter he toiled. Sometimes fatigue would make him turn aside and rest for a few days with some kindly person from whom he could get food and drink and on whose premises he could sleep all he needed to, and where his sore pads could get a chance to heal. Then on he would go again, still in the general direction of home, and keeping up his journey until once more weariness and starvation made him take another rest.

He used brain, as well as courage and wiry strength, on that tremendous journey of his, never traveling too far at any one stretch to render himself permanently lame or enfeebled. It was only on the last lap of his journey that he allowed his keen longing for his master to make him careless of fatigue and hunger. For as he neared Silverton, Bobbie forgot caution and put on all the remaining speed he had. He had been lost at Wolcott, Indiana, on August 15, 1923. On February 15, 1924, exactly six months later, he staggered into Silverton and to his master's house. His three-thousand-mile wanderings were over.

Worn to a skeleton, his feet bleeding and torn, his weariness so great that he could not stand up for days, he had found his way home—home to the master for whom he had been searching so steadfastly for a half year and across three thousand miles of mountain and desert and unknown country.

At once news of Bobbie's exploit was telegraphed everywhere. Then

The Three-Thousand-Mile Collie

began an ordeal almost as tiring as had been his journey. People flocked by thousands to see the wonderful dog. They patted him until his tender skin was bruised. They brought him ridiculous gifts by the dozen—gifts that any dog would have swapped gladly for a pound of raw steak.

A model bungalow was built as a home for him. He received a gold collar, and a handful of medals, and many another tribute to his brain and courage. A public reception was held in his honor, at which the wholesale patting and mauling were so painful that Brazier rigged up a wire screen between the great dog and his over-enthusiastic admirers.

From the statements of people with whom Bobbie stopped or by whom he was seen on his trip, it seems that at first he cast about in a wide arc of almost a thousand miles, before he could get his bearings and start on a straighter line for home.

Not long after he got back to Silverton, he created another and slighter stir in local newspapers by turning aside from his daily walk and galloping around a pile of underbrush, barking at the top of his lungs. The pile of brush was investigated, and the body of a suicide was found beneath it.

SPORT
A Battle with Wolves for a Baby's Life

HE WAS a big and formidable dog of no one breed. His name was Sport. He belonged to Andre Minnett, a prosperous woodsman who lived at Seguin Falls in Ontario, Canada. The huge dog used to go with his master on trapping journeys through the forests, guarding the man's slumbers by the campfire at night, and more than once tackling and thrashing a wolf that prowled too close to the camp.

Sport was an inspired wolf fighter. Perhaps in his mixed ancestry there was a goodly share of wolf blood. For he used his brain even more than his size and strength in these fights, outmaneuvering the most crafty of his foes at their own tactics. Sport's renown as a wolf killer spread far and wide. The average timber wolf is more than a match for the average dog of his size. But Sport combined within himself all the elements which make a wolf such a terrible adversary.

Minnett knew, of course, that if the dog should go far into the forests, alone, and there encounter a pack of several wolves, he would be torn to pieces by them, and all his prowess would not avail against their greater numbers. But Sport was too clever to take a suicidal chance like that. He kept reasonably close to his master during those forest camping trips. He was fearless, but he was not a fool.

There came a rival to Minnett in Sport's affections. Indeed this rival soon supplanted the master and everyone else in the dog's heart. This newcomer was Minnett's baby son, Jean. Almost from the hour of Baby Jean's birth, Sport was the child's worshiping slave. The dog would sit or lie by the hour beside the youngster's crib or peram-

A Battle with Wolves for a Baby's Life

bulator. No stranger could come anywhere near to Jean. The dog was his tireless guard as well as his playmate. Hanging tight to the dog's mighty shoulder, Jean took his own first tottering steps. He mauled and hauled Sport around in delight. From no grown-up except his master and mistress would the dog have permitted such liberties. But he reveled in them when they were perpetrated by his idolized Jean. He grew to grudge the once-welcome camping tours, since they kept him away from the child for days at a time. Mrs. Minnett felt her baby's safety was amply assured, even in that wilderness region of savage beasts, while Sport was on guard over him.

The Minnett house stood in a clearing in the woods. One day Minnett went up to a hilltop not far away to cut logs. Mrs. Minnett took advantage of the morning's unusual warmth to put Jean in his perambulator and wheel him out into a patch of sunshine in the yard. Then she went back to her housework, leaving the kitchen door open so she could hear the child if he should call to her. As usual, Sport stretched himself out on the ground beside the baby carriage. Of old, he would have gone up the hill with his master to watch the wood chopping. But nowadays the dog never stirred willingly from Jean.

From where Minnett was working, the baby carriage and its occupant were cut off from view by a corner of the house. So was Sport. Minnett did not know his wife had taken the baby out into the yard, but supposed he was playing comfortably indoors. Otherwise he would have been more excited when he saw three large and hungry wolves slinking down the hillside toward the clearing. He knew they would not be able to get into the house to harm his wife or Jean, and he knew Sport could be relied on to chase them away. In broad daylight and so close to human habitation, they were not likely to attack the formidable dog.

A Battle with Wolves for a Baby's Life

So he watched carelessly their furtive advance down the wooded hill and toward the clearing, wondering, with no special interest, what hope of food could induce them to venture there at such a sunlit hour.

Sport was roused from his cozy nap beside the perambulator by a scent he knew and hated. He sprang to his feet and saw the three oncoming wolves. He knew well, from his woodland experiences, that no one dog could hope to thrash three timber wolves. Behind him was the open doorway of the house. Into it he could easily run for shelter, and could give the alarm which would bring Mrs. Minnett to the rescue. But before she or her husband could possibly be made to understand what was amiss, the three savage beasts could readily snatch up the helpless baby from the carriage, and either drag him off with them into the forest or else tear his throat out. No, there was but one thing for Sport to do. And he did it.

He ran forward to meet the invaders, keeping his own body always between them and Jean. He had his line of campaign all figured out, as later developments proved. This must be no furious dash at the wolves, which would let two of the wily brutes engage him in battle while the third seized the baby and made off with it or killed it in the carriage. He must fight with his brain as never before. And he did.

Minnett saw the wolves advance a little way into the clearing. Then he saw Sport run toward them from that part of the yard which could not be seen from the hilltop. Next he watched the beginning of a strange combat.

I am going to tell you of the fight in the words of the Montreal correspondent of the London *Daily Express*. He was one of several Canadian newspaper men to whom Minnett described what followed.

"The dog sparred like a prize fighter with his snarling opponents.

A Battle with Wolves for a Baby's Life

After edging about for a minute or so, Sport had the wolves with their backs to the baby, and he himself was edging off into the woods. Dog and wolves alike seemed afraid to strike the first blow. Then, suddenly, Sport turned tail to his foes and dashed off into the forest, as if in terror. The three gray-coated wolves followed hard at his heels. The dog never returned.

"But he had accomplished what he had endeavored to do: he had led the wolves away from the baby's perambulator. Mr. Minnett says Sport could easily have sought protection within the kitchen doorway, but that he seemed to realize that this would put the baby in mortal danger."

So much for the newspaper account of the drama. To me it is a splendid story of sacrifice and of the love that gladly throws life away for the sake of saving another from harm.

Many dogs would have dashed forth bravely to battle, as did Sport. But few would have used such brain work in luring the wolves away from the child. A grand tale of a grand dog!

KARROO
The Terrier Named for a Desert

AN ITALIAN scientific expedition, under command of Attilib Gatti, was on its way from Capetown, South Africa, to Cairo. In the dreariest section of the dreary Karroo Desert, Gatti happened to see a grimy white object lying in the sand. It was a dog—a thoroughbred fox terrier. The poor creature was at the point of death from starvation and thirst. Never did anyone discover to whom the terrier had belonged or what he was doing in such an outlandish place. He was a dog of mystery.

Gatti gave him food and water, and nursed him back to health. Then, as he could not abandon the animal, he attached him to the expedition, naming him Karroo, after the desert in which he had been found. That was the beginning of a close friendship between Gatti and the terrier.

Karroo was civil to all the members of the party, but from the outset he chose Gatti as his master. He earned his way over and over again in giving the alarm at night when marauding natives prowled around the camp looking for a chance to steal. Karroo could hear their softest tread far off, and was on the alert at once, barking fiercely until everyone was awake.

Gatti went out into the hills, during a few days' rest, to get fresh meat for the caravan. Karroo trotted proudly along with his master. An enormous gnu broke cover. Gatti fired. The gnu rolled over. The man turned to signal to the camp for a cart to come up for the game. Just then, Karroo burst into crazy barking. Gatti turned. The gnu

The Terrier Named for a Desert

had merely been knocked over by the bullet which had grazed its scalp. Now it was on its feet again, and was charging furiously, head down.

Gatti did not have time to raise his gun and fire again, or to leap to one side to dodge the charge. It was Karroo who gave him his chance. In an account written for *The Tail-Wagger Magazine*, Gatti described what followed:

"Karroo hurled himself at the gnu's head, and bounced in the air like a rubber ball, from the sharp impact of a powerful horn. But the charge of the beast had been stopped for a fraction of a second, giving me just the time to dispatch it with a second shot, thereby saving myself from a nasty injury."

This was not the only time the heroic little fox terrier stood between his master and peril. The expedition was in Rhodesia. A camp site was chosen in an ideally sheltered spot near the edge of a towering pile of rocks. But the moment the first tent peg was driven, Karroo began to yelp and to dance around in wild excitement, as though he were trying to warn his human friends against camping there. Gatti bade him be quiet; and the work went on.

But, after the camp was pitched and the party were getting ready for dinner, Karroo set up such a frenzy of barks that Gatti came out of his tent to see what was the matter. He was in time to see a gigantic python crawling out of the pile of rocks and starting for the tent. In front of the serpent danced Karroo, still barking the alarm and making snarling dashes at the advancing foe. The python paused, as if puzzled by the antics of the raging dog. This gave Gatti time to run back into the tent for his rifle, and to send a bullet through the snake's head.

But Karroo was not yet satisfied. He sniffed at the dead snake, then ran over to the rocks and began to bark louder than ever. Nor

Social Climbers   Diana Thorne

The Terrier Named for a Desert

could he be silenced. For once he disobeyed orders, and continued to rush from one end of the rocks to the other, still barking frantically.

At last Gatti was so impressed by the terrier's endless warnings that he ordered cans of gasoline to be poured into the crevices of the rock pile and over the top of it, and set alight.

Up swirled the yellow-red flames. Fire spurted out on every side. But more than mere fire came out of these rock crevices. Driven forth by the blaze, seven pythons crawled from the lair.

Karroo was for tackling all seven of them. But Gatti caught him by the collar and dragged him out of harm's way, while others of the party emptied their rifles into the squirming creatures.

Presently, all seven pythons were shot to death. The smallest of them was eighteen feet long.

The ground was examined. It was found that Gatti's tent had been pitched in the middle of a runway used by the snakes when they issued forth from their lairs for the night's hunting.

But for Karroo's frantic warning, Gatti might have been the central figure, that night, in a rather hideous tragedy.

For an entire year Karroo was a loved and honored member of the party. For an entire year he appointed himself perpetual guard of the ever-moving camp. Then, one night, a lion came creeping around the outermost radius of the camp fire. With his usual challenge bark, Karroo charged out to meet the invader. Before Gatti could interfere or call him back, the plucky terrier was at close quarters with the enemy so many times larger and stronger than himself. A blow of the lion's great paw killed him.

So ended the gaily courageous life of a true hero-dog, a life he had risked again and again and again for mankind.

LORY THE LURID
A Right Disreputable Dog

LORY has been written of, many times, in the newspapers of Great Britain. But the Glasgow *News* described him best when it spoke of him as "Lory the Lurid."

A right disreputable dog was Lory. For all I know, he may still be living. If he is, I hazard the guess that he is still lurid and still disreputable; and that his misdeeds are still giving a bad name to all local dogdom.

The full tale of his adventures would fill many pages of this book, so I am going to touch on only a few of the high spots of his career—just enough to give you a general idea what the rest of it is like.

In the first place, Lory was an Old English sheepdog. Most of you have seen dogs of this breed at shows and elsewhere. They are silver-gray and white, practically tailless and with enormous silken coats which take most of one man's time to keep combed and clean.

These dogs are wise and beautiful and staunch. During the World War, they won deathless renown as couriers and as helpers for the wounded. Brush back the avalanche of hair that covers their eyes, and you will find those eyes are sagacious and steadfast. A great breed of dog; and too little appreciated.

Lory was a show-type dog, and was valuable. That is why his owner, Miss Doherty, of 342 Paisley Road, Glasgow, Scotland, was willing to pay a reward for his return after each of his wanderings from home. And these wanderings were many.

Lory had a craving to wander along the line of docks, and to make

A Right Disreputable Dog

friends with sailors who happened to be in port just then. Sometimes these sailors stole him—with his own rowdy consent—and held him for ransom. Sometimes things went a bit further. For instance:

On one of Lory's rambles along the docks he followed a group of sailors into a public house. There one of the men decided it would be an amusing stunt to get the dog drunk.

The average dog has no use for liquor. Its pungent smell and its fiery taste disgust him. But Lory was not an average dog. The day was hot and he was thirsty. So when a sailor set on the floor a big bowl of ale, plentifully laced with gin, Lory drank greedily every drop of it. Then he proceeded to get very drunk indeed.

He staggered sideways out into the street, and gave such a disgraceful exhibition of intoxication that the police slung him into a patrol wagon and carried him to headquarters on suspicion that he had hydrophobia.

There he would have been shot at once—for hydrophobia (or rabies) has been stamped out in Great Britain and there is always a dread lest it reappear—had not the police surgeon gotten a whiff of his alcoholic breath, and guessed what was really the matter. So Lory was put into a cell and allowed to sleep off his potations. After which, Miss Doherty, on her round of the various pounds and stations for news of her valuable dog, found him and paid to have him set free and taken home again.

On several other occasions and for several other misdemeanors, Lory fell into the hands of the police and was bailed out by his mistress. Soon every policeman as well as every sailor and dog-thief in Glasgow was acquainted with him; and much was the profit which some of them derived from rescuing him from scrapes and taking him home.

A Right Disreputable Dog

But his crowning achievement came when he boarded a steamship lying at its dock, in Glasgow, and stowed away until after the vessel had sailed. Several of the sailors recognized him. More than one of them were old friends and fellow-revelers of his. They made him welcome on the long voyage to New York, knowing they would reap a rich reward from Miss Doherty if they could bring him safely back to her in Glasgow after the voyage.

Lory had a beautiful time at sea. He was the life of the ship, and he got into mischief on every possible occasion. But as the vessel steamed into New York harbor, the dog seemed to decide against the chance of becoming an American citizen.

He waxed restless. When the ship was near her anchorage, he jumped overboard. Every effort was made by his sailor friends to save him. But the captain refused to waste time in searching for an animal which had become a pest, and the sailors gave him up for lost. There was much sorrow among them, not only over losing the chance of a fat reward from Miss Doherty but because the dog's ragamuffin ways had endeared him to them.

One of the crew got shore leave next day. He decided to visit Bedloe's Island, and to climb the Statue of Liberty. So he boarded the boat which carries passengers to the Statue from the Battery.

As the boat docked at Bedloe's Island, Lory frisked forward to welcome him. Evidently he had swum ashore to the island after he jumped overboard. There he had made himself perfectly at home. And now he was delighted to see his sailor friend.

The sailor collared him, and carried him back to New York and smuggled him aboard the ship. He and his mates kept Lory safely hidden from the officers until the vessel started on her return trip.

A Right Disreputable Dog

After a double crossing of the Atlantic Ocean, Lory was restored to his owner; and the sailors received a big sum of money for his return. The much-traveled animal might have been expected to rest peacefully at home after such a prolonged adventure. But that was not Lory's way.

Inside of a month he was back along the docks. Once more a convivial group of sailors invited him into a public house for a bowl of ale-and-gin. And once more, a few hours later, Miss Doherty was informed over the telephone by a police sergeant:

"Madam, your dog is locked up in the cells again. 'Drunk and incapable.' Please come down here for him at once."

Do you wonder the Glasgow *News* referred to him as "Lory the Lurid"?

REX
Missing for Six Weeks

REX was a big police dog owned by J. V. Pappas, a florist, of 61 West Twenty-seventh Street, New York City. Once, when Rex was absent from the store, two holdup men came in. They drew automatic pistols, and they made Pappas and his assistant stand still while the money drawer was robbed of two hundred twenty-five dollars.

The thieves escaped so easily and with such good plunder that they decided to rob the store again. So, a couple of months later, they came back for more loot. This time Rex was in the store, but he had just been shut in a closet where he was accustomed to sleep at night. So, when the two holdup men appeared, he could not be of any help at all to his master.

Pappas and his assistant tried to put up a fight, but the gunmen fired several shots which scared them into submission. Then the marauders proceeded to rifle the till.

The shots had aroused Rex to a fury of excitement. In vain he hurled his wiry body against the unyielding panels of the door of the closet where he was imprisoned. He filled the air with his growls and roars of rage. But that was all the good it did. However, the instant the thieves left the store, Pappas flung open the door of the closet and shouted, "After them, Rex! *Get* them!"

The big dog did not wait for a second command. Snarling in rabid fury, he dashed out into the street as the robbers were scrambling into the car they had left with engine running in front of the floral shop.

They slammed the door in Rex's face as he charged murderously

Missing for Six Weeks

at them. The car set off at high speed through the crowded street. Rex continued to leap against the door of the car, until the pace grew too hot for him. Then he chased the machine, in and out of traffic, keeping close behind it. This much Pappas and his assistant saw from the doorway of the shop. And that was all. They waited for hours. Rex did not come back.

Six weeks passed. No sign of the missing dog.

Then one evening, at closing time, there was a wild scratching at the shop door. It was opened and in galloped Rex and flung himself adoringly upon his master. The dog was bone-thin. His coat was covered with mud. He was wildly excited.

That's all there is to the story. Where had Rex been all those six weeks? Had he caught the thieves? What had happened? It is all a mystery—just another mystery of a wise and loyal dog.

GENGISK
The Dog Who Saved a King

IN THE beautiful gardens of the royal palace Sans Souci, the favorite abode of Frederick the Great, King of Prussia, stands (or stood) an elaborate monument erected by the monarch to mark the burial place of his dog, Gengisk. It was not mere sentiment which led the grim old warrior king to put this stone over the grave of a dog, for Gengisk had saved Frederick's life and liberty and perhaps had thus helped to change the history of Europe. Here is the story:

Frederick was at war with Russia. He had lifted the Prussian kingdom from its somewhat low position and had made it one of the great powers of Europe. All this Frederick had done through his own genius. Had he died or been taken prisoner by any of his various enemies, his newly raised kingdom might well have fallen back into mediocrity, and the future of all Europe might have been altered.

On every campaign Frederick was accompanied by his Great Dane dog Gengisk, a powerful and gigantic brute that was utterly devoted to his royal master and was gifted with a queer psychic sense which warned him when Frederick was in danger.

Frederick used to play with Gengisk in rough romping fashion that scandalized his stiffly dignified court. He nursed the dog personally through several illnesses. A foreign emissary was sent once to see the king and to report to his enemies what Frederick was doing. The emissary returned with the report that he had found the king sitting on the floor of his throne room, feeding his dog beef bones from a tin basin. But Gengisk repaid well this royal favor, as you shall see.

Great Dane   Diana Thorne

Setter Retrieving   Diana Thorne

The Dog Who Saved a King

It was during Frederick's war with Russia that he was riding along a strip of deserted ground, on his way from one division of his army to another. He was paying a "surprise visit" of inspection to this second army, and he was riding alone, except for Gengisk. Scouts had reported that the enemy were many miles away. There seemed no need for an armed body of men to accompany Frederick.

As Frederick was nearing the edge of a stream that ran through a bit of woodland, Gengisk halted, sniffing the air. Suddenly the huge dog dashed to the head of Frederick's horse, and nipped at the steed's nostrils and chest, striving frantically to bring him to a standstill. The horse merely shied, and continued his journey. Finding he could not stop the charger, Gengisk leaped up at the king, driving his curved fangs into Frederick's thick riding boots and seeking to drag him from the saddle.

A lesser man, or a man who knew less of dogs, might readily have kicked Gengisk aside and kept on. But Frederick had had experience with the Great Dane's odd psychic premonitions. So instead of kicking or lashing the dog, he brought his horse to a halt and dismounted.

At once Gengisk ceased to snap and leap at him, and stood stock still. The king looked about him, but could see nothing to account for Gengisk's strange behavior. He turned, as if to remount his horse. Instantly, the dog barred his way, shivering in a fever of eagerness.

The king knelt down, with his ear to the ground. Faintly he could hear the distant thud of hundreds of horses' hoofs. A Cossack raiding party was coming directly toward him, hidden from sight by the intervening woods. Should they catch a glimpse of him, he must inevitably be captured or killed. His horse was tired, and he could not hope to escape. Leading the weary steed, Frederick hurried to the edge of the

The Dog Who Saved a King

stream and took refuge under one of the arches of the bridge, in a thicket of undergrowth.

A minute or two later, the Cossacks came riding over the bridge above his head. The Great Dane growled. To keep Gengisk silent, Frederick gripped the dog's mighty jaws between his own hands until the last of the riders had passed on.

Some time later, at the battle of Soor, Frederick's camp fell into the hands of the Russians. The king had left Gengisk in the royal tent when he himself went forth to the field. Thus, the great dog was captured. Everyone had heard of Gengisk and of Frederick's devotion to him and of the way in which he had warned the unguarded monarch of the approach of the Cossack raiding party. So, instead of shooting the dog, his captors carried him to Russian headquarters. There he was given to General Nodosti, who in turn gave the magnificent brute to his wife as one of the precious spoils of war.

There was talk of holding Gengisk as a hostage, or of exchanging him for some imprisoned Russian of high rank. For a time the dog became one of the important pawns in the iron game of war and of statecraft. But the Russian general, Rotherberg, intervened. Either through diplomacy or because he also was a dog man, he sent Gengisk back to Frederick.

The Prussian king was pacing his study at Sans Souci when Gengisk was brought to him. The dog leaped upon his master, licking the monarch's face and making the room re-echo with his barks of joy. Frederick broke down and wept like a child whose lost pet is restored. From that time on, until Gengisk's death, the dog and his master were never again separated for a single week.

FANG

The Seventeenth Century Dog Detective

ON THE Kentish shore of the river Thames in England is a patch of land known once as Dog's Island and now corrupted in title to The Isle of Dogs. Old legends say that when this bit of ground was really an island, many hundreds of years ago, it was infested with savage wild dogs. But it took its original name, Dog's Island, in quite a different way.

Somewhere around the middle of the seventeenth century, a Kentish squire named Alexander Iden lived on the mainland just opposite this isle. He is said to have been descended from "Alexander Iden, a poor esquire of Kent," who killed the rebel, Jack Cade, during the reign of Henry VI of England.

Iden noticed a great Irish wolfhound hiding in the shrubbery at the edge of his grounds. He noticed, too, that two or three times a day the dog would swim across to the island and would disappear into the dense thickets which covered it. Day after day and week after week this same thing happened.

Iden became keenly interested in the wolfhound's odd behavior. He made inquiries. Nobody could tell him to whom the big dog belonged or where he came from or why he swam across to the island several times a day and hid amid its thickets. But a tenant farmer said the dog had stopped daily for a few minutes at his cottage, and there had received a dish of table scraps. As soon as the animal had bolted this food, he would set off for the island. The farmer had named him Fang, a common name in early England for large dogs.

The Seventeenth Century Dog Detective

Iden became still more interested. He made friends with the dog, and gave him a heaping dish of food every day. The dog would eat the dinner eagerly, then would offer his forepaw to Iden to shake, and set out at once to swim the river.

One day Iden had a rowboat ready. When the dog began his swim, the squire followed close behind him in the boat. Fang paid no attention. Iden was his friend, and he did not seem to feel any interest in avoiding pursuit.

As Fang disappeared in the island bushes, Iden was at his heels. The dog moved on through the dense undergrowth for some little distance, with Iden behind him. Man and dog came out into a small clearing in the center of the island. There the ground evidently had been dug up, not many months before, in a lozenge-shaped patch about six feet long and three feet wide. Fang went straight to this spot and lay down. His chin rested on the ground, and he seemed grief-stricken. For perhaps an hour he lay thus. Then, still paying no attention to the wondering Iden, he trotted back to the river and swam across once more to the mainland.

It was for the sake of lying unhappily alongside the oblong of upturned earth that Fang had been swimming to the island two or three times a day, for months. Iden decided to go further into the mystery.

So he rowed back to his own home and called for two of his laborers to bring shovels and return with him to the island. There the men dug into the upturned ground in the tiny clearing. When they had delved to a depth of four feet they unearthed the body of a man.

The body was well dressed, but the skull had been fractured as if by a heavy blow. There could be no doubt the man had been murdered

The Seventeenth Century Dog Detective

and that his body had been carried secretly to this hidden spot and there had been buried.

Iden had the victim taken to the mainland and buried with church rites in the nearest graveyard. Then he took Fang home with him.

The wolfhound was obedient and even affectionate toward his new master. Yet, every day, once or twice, he continued to swim the river and lie mournfully beside the empty grave of the murdered man. Nor did he abate the air of grief that was his. Iden thought a change of scene might make Fang forget this unhappy daily vigil. So, on his own next journey to London, he took the dog with him. Fang went along, obediently but sorrowfully. Iden saw to it that he could not escape and find his way back to the grave.

They spent some weeks in London. Iden made a number of purchases, and decided to ship them back to his Kentish home by water. He went down to the river-front one day with Fang, as always, at his heels. There he bargained with boatmen for the transporting of his purchases. While he was engaged in this chaffering, a boat came toward the slip. It was rowed by a professional riverman, who had seen the stranger talking with his fellow river-porters and who hoped to come in for a share of the freighting.

The man stepped ashore at the wharf. But before he had taken two steps forward, Fang gave a wild-beast roar, and launched himself at the newcomer's throat. The giant dog bore the man to the ground, and was seeking to tear out his jugular when Iden intervened.

Iden was a man who thought quickly. Also he understood dogs. Fang was gentle and friendly with everyone, in spite of the eternal sadness that enveloped him. Then why had this friendly hound flown so murderously at an inoffensive stranger? To Iden's way of thinking, there was

The Seventeenth Century Dog Detective

only one sane explanation. It was a clue that seemed to him well worth following. He called for the police and bade them seize the mishandled riverman. Then, holding Fang by the collar, Iden commanded the man to confess, under penalty of having the homicidal brute turned loose upon him again.

In mortal terror at sight of the ravening jaws and the glaring eyes of the infuriated dog, the man blubbered out a confession that he had murdered Fang's master and had buried him on that desolate island in the Thames.

Whether Fang had witnessed the murder or whether he merely recognized the riverman as a former enemy of his master's, nobody knows. But he had attacked him on sight, he who was so friendly with most humans.

The murderer was brought before the London magistrates, and, a few days later, was hanged. Hangings were public in that age. And Iden took Fang along to witness the punishment of his master's slayer.

The odd part of the tale is that when Fang returned to Iden's home in Kent, he did not visit the empty grave again, and he cast off the sadness that had been his for so long. He seemed to realize that justice at last had been done, and that his master was avenged.

PEGEEN
The Dog Who Learned to Reason

PEGEEN lived in Ireland nearly a century ago. As a puppy she was wild and disobedient. So her master, a merchant in the city of Cork, bought a whipstock—one of those long hickory gads which were used for ox-driving. And he used it unsparingly on her, in his effort to turn her into a decent canine citizen. Pegeen took a strong dislike to this ox-gad, and she determined to put it somewhere out of her master's reach.

Three times she carried it far away and hid it. Three times it was found again, and Pegeen was made to feel its sting, for her sin in stealing it. The fourth time she crept to her master's room at night. There she found the whipstock and crawled stealthily out of the room with it. A member of the household saw her and followed her as she slipped through an open window to the street.

Several farmhands were coming along the sidewalk. Pegeen laid the gad in a conspicuous place in the middle of the pavement. Then she retreated. The men arrived at the spot where it lay. One of them picked it up and carried it off with him. Pegeen, from behind the hedge, wagged her tail delightedly at this final disappearance of her wooden enemy.

Pegeen's meals always were served to her in an ornamental tin pail, with a handle to it, such as children use for filling with sand at the seashore. She loved that pail. One day, a child passed the house on his way to the beach, carrying just such a pail. Pegeen caught sight of it, and dashed furiously out into the road. She snatched the pail by the handle, yanked it away from the astonished child, and bolted indoors

The Dog Who Learned to Reason

with it. There she saw her own pail in its usual place. She glared in unbelieving amazement from the stolen pail to her own. Then she dropped the pail she had snatched, and slunk away in shame to the cellar.

Another trick of Pegeen's—one which she taught herself to perform without any human's tuition—was to follow kind-looking people in the street, and fawn upon them and stand on her hind legs and then sit and beg. This she would do until a penny was tossed to her. Picking up the coin daintily between her teeth, she would trot off to a baker in the neighborhood and lay it on his shop counter. The man would give her a penny's worth of cake or a bun. She would swallow this at one mouthful and then trot forth again on another begging expedition.

Pegeen grew to great size, and in time she acquired a solemn dignity which was far different from her early rowdyism. She was her master's day-and-night comrade, and guarded his house and grounds right zealously from intruders.

Her new dignity was amusing in its lofty solemnity. She seemed to have settled down into a perfect house dog, and to have put behind her all her former pranks. No longer did she condescend to beg for pennies, nor did she make herself a neighborhood pest.

But there was one dog in the same street which refused to be impressed by Pegeen's new air of stateliness. This was a lap dog which, in puppyhood, had been wont to romp gaily with her, and which could not be made to understand that her hoydenish days were past. Always he would scamper out when he saw her pacing majestically down the street, and would try in vain to incite her to a romp.

This used to mortify Pegeen, and she would try to ignore him, the more so if passers-by happened to laugh at the two.

The Inconsolable   Diana Thorne

The Dog Who Learned to Reason

One morning the climax came. Pegeen was on her daily walk, when the lap dog galloped forth to intercept her. As she paid no attention to his antics, he lost his temper, and nipped her sharply in the hind foot.

This was too much of an indignity to be borne. Pegeen would not lower herself by thrashing her tormentor, but there were other ways of teaching him his place. Stooping, she caught him by the nape of the neck. This without checking her stately stride.

On she moved, carrying the lap dog thus in spite of his howls and twistings. Presently she came to the bay. Out to the end of the longest pier she paced, the lap dog still held with gentle firmness between her powerful jaws. At the end of the pier she leaned far over and dropped him into the water.

Down went the victim, deep under the surface. Pegeen watched in quiet amusement his wild struggles as he rose. But her amusement changed to worry, as she saw the poor little fellow splashing helplessly about, too weak to make headway against the strong ebb-tide.

Instantly her dignity and her resentment were forgotten. She dived far out into the water. Coming up, she swam to where the lap dog was feebly trying to keep afloat. Seizing him once more by the nape of the neck, she swam for the nearest patch of beach.

There she carried him high up on dry land, and set him gently on his feet. The lap dog set off for home at top speed, ki-yi-ing in mortal terror, while Pegeen continued her dignified morning walk.

"It would be difficult," wrote Dr. Abell, of Cork, in describing the scene as an eye-witness, "to conceive of any punishment more aptly contrived, or more complete in character."

I agree with him.

TRICK
A Lurcher with a Queer History

TRICK'S story has been written several times and from several angles. For in his day he was a celebrity. Perhaps the best account of him was Walter M. Gallachin's in *The Tail-Wagger Magazine*. It is to this account that I owe some of the most worth-while of the following incidents.

Near the New Forest, in Hampshire, England, lived a tenant farmer, Hugh Trotman, who was an ardent sportsman. One day he shot a grouse that fell into a field that was choked with thick brambles and undergrowth. Trotman searched the field in vain for the slain bird.

As he returned toward the road from his fruitless search, he saw a man lounging against a tree, watching him. Beside the man sat a shabby-looking dog, a lurcher. Trotman recognized the dog's master as a well-known local poacher and all-around loafer who went by the nickname of Gypsy Jake.

"Can't find the bird?" called Jake. "Wait a bit. My tyke here will retrieve him for you. Trick! Get him!"

At the command, Trick darted into the field. In less than a minute he returned and laid the dead grouse at Jake's feet. The work had been so swiftly and so perfectly done that Trotman asked several questions about Trick.

He learned that the dog was expert in every form of gun work, and had not his equal at coursing hares. Jake finished the tale by saying he himself was dead broke and wanted to raise some cash in a hurry. He offered to sell Trick for three pounds sterling (then worth not quite

A Lurcher with a Queer History

fifteen dollars in our American money). Trotman beat him down to two pounds, and bought Trick.

The lurcher was wholly willing to leave his old master for his new owner. Before long, Trotman began to realize that he had made the best bargain of his life in getting such a dog at two pounds, or indeed at any price at all. For the lurcher had learned not only to hunt, but to do many other lucrative things.

The English gypsies of a few decades ago were of a wholly different type from the gypsies of our country. They had more tricks for catching landowners' game and for devious forms of trickery than perhaps any other class of people on earth. And they trained their lurchers—a cur supposed to have been originally a cross between a sheepdog and a greyhound—to do unbelievable things. If I had lived in those days and had wanted a supernaturally gifted and educated dog, I should have bought a lurcher puppy and hired some skilled English gypsy to train him for me.

Trick not only was the best field dog Trotman ever had owned or seen, but he used to bring home plump hares and pheasants which he had caught. He carried these so tenderly that they were unharmed. Sometimes he varied such fare by bringing to his master a few chickens or geese from neighboring farms. Gypsy Jake had taught him right shrewdly. The dog did not eat or even injure the birds and rabbits he brought home. All of them were laid at the feet of Trotman. Also Trick never barked, nor made any sound at all. And he moved as warily and silently as a wolf.

He used to trot alongside the farmer's cart, on the weekly trips to the near-by market town or to Lyndhurst. On the first of these trips, Trotman noticed a new phase of the training which Gypsy Jake had given the lurcher. Every time a policeman would come in sight, Trick

A Lurcher with a Queer History

would disappear. Nor would he rejoin the cart until it had traveled for another quarter mile or so. Jake had taught him to do this, lest the poaching dog and the poaching gypsy become associated with each other in the minds of the police. Also, when Trotman was on the streets of a town or was talking to other people, the dog would pay no attention to him, but would keep out of sight. This was another bit of teaching which the crafty Jake had imparted to him.

In a dozen ways Trick showed the devious training that had been his. Some of these things amused Trotman. Some of them horrified him—as when neighbors' livestock were brought home by the dog—and still others won him much renown among Hampshire sportsmen.

Far and wide went the story of Trick's prowess in the field. It came at last to the ears of Colonel Desmond, who was Trotman's landlord and a devotee of sport. Desmond asked Trotman to sell him the dog. Trotman happened to be in need of ready money just then. Also he wanted to oblige his landlord. So he sold Trick to Colonel Desmond for twenty pounds—just ten times as much as Trotman himself had paid for the lurcher.

But just a little while before that, a woman had called on Trotman and introduced herself as Gypsy Jake's wife. She said her husband was desperately ill, and the family was without food. She begged Trotman to lend Trick to her for one month.

At the end of the month she returned the lurcher, and told Trotman that Trick had saved the whole family from starving. During that time, the dog had brought home to Gypsy Jake's hovel thirty-one rabbits, seventeen hares, a partridge, two wild ducks and three pheasants. Truly the lurcher had paid his way, by game thefts, while he was visiting his first master.

A Lurcher with a Queer History

Colonel Desmond was invited by a neighboring landowner to a duck shoot, to be held on a grand scale, each guest to bring along his own retriever. Desmond accepted. But when he appeared at the shoot with the shabby lurcher slinking at his heels, a laugh went up.

Trick was a sorry sight, indeed, compared with the thoroughbred dogs of the host and of the other guests. But Desmond knew what he could do. As the laughter and the guying died down, he offered calmly to bet ten pounds apiece with his host and with any guests, that Trick would retrieve more shot ducks from the water that day than any other dog in the party.

When his hearers realized that Desmond was not joking, they fell over one another in their efforts to take the bets. It looked like ridiculously easy money for each of the takers. The keepers grinned broadly, and prepared to get much secret fun out of the wretched exhibition which poor Trick was due to make among all those splendidly trained thoroughbred retrievers.

The grins were soon wiped from their faces, and from those of the sportsmen who had wagered ten pounds apiece on the result. For Trick got into action immediately. He sighted the fallen birds sooner and swam for them with far greater speed than did the best of his competitors. All day he was scarcely ever out of the water, except to lay a retrieved duck in front of Desmond and then to plunge back after the next victim of the guns.

Desmond won all his bets, with many birds to spare. Trick was easy victor over the best of the thoroughbreds. From that time on, in Hampshire sportsman circles, his name was immortal.

HECTOR
The Mischief Dog

IN THE Scotch Highlands dwelt James Hogg, poet and shepherd, known far and near for his quaint writings and for the true stories he told of his collies. In his books and letters and in his *Shepherd's Calendar,* he described the lives and adventures of these canine chums of his. Foremost among them was his "mischief dog," Hector.

When Hector was still less than a year old, Hogg took him one bitterly cold day to a farm at Shorthope to drive back a bunch of lambs to the home farm. The winter day closed in darkness before the flock could be gotten home. When they were near their destination, the whole bunch broke and scattered in confusion.

Master and dog worked for an hour to collect the strays. Then Hogg went into the house, certain that every one of the lambs had been driven safely into the fold. He called Hector to come in with him out of the cold, but the dog did not obey. Indeed, Hector was nowhere to be found.

At daylight next morning, Hogg went out to look for the missing collie. He had not far to search. There, at one of the two gates of the fold, sat Hector, the frost white on his coat. There he had sat all night long, hungry and chilly.

Hogg had driven the lambs through the gate into the enclosure and then shut the gate. In the darkness he had not seen that the second gate of the fold was wide open. But Hector had seen. The collie had known the uneasy lambs would find the opening and would scatter out through it into the night, and be lost, or stolen, or killed by wild

The Mischief Dog

animals. So he had sat down in the doorway of the fold, and had stayed there all night, keeping every lamb from getting out.

The young dog's chief joy in life was to crouch menacingly in front of the family cat, as if about to pounce at her. As a matter of fact, he never did pounce; and he even consented to share his dinner dish with her. But he was always threatening.

One morning Hogg had guests in the house and assembled them in the living-room for family prayers before breakfast. Their seats all happened to face a rug on which the cat was lying. Just as they knelt down to pray, Hector trotted into the room.

He saw them all apparently crouching around the cat. With a loud bark of delight, he joined in the supposed sport, dashing about among the kneeling worshipers as if exhorting them to pounce at the cat, and then crouching threateningly, himself, in front of her.

Many shepherds in the Highlands used to take their collies to church with them, the well-trained dogs lying quietly at their masters' feet all through the long service. They still do so. But Hogg dared not take Hector there. For, as soon as Hogg began to take part in the congregational singing of hymns or of psalms, Hector would join in, screeching at the top of his lungs. Hogg wrote: "The shepherds hid their heads . . . . . on the backs of the seats . . . . . and the lasses looked down to the ground and laughed till their faces grew red."

Hogg was planning a visit to a distant farm near Bowerhope, and he decided not to take Hector along. He had done so once before, and the dog had disgraced him by picking quarrels with every cur he met along the road, so that the journey had been one endless succession of dog fights. There had been threats of shooting and of damage suits, and more than one angry farmer had threatened to thrash Hogg be-

The Mischief Dog

cause Hector had thrashed the farmer's dog. The trip had not been pleasant for anyone but Hector.

So when Hogg contemplated the trip the following year he told his mother at supper one night that he was going to start on the long pedestrian journey to Bowerhope at sunrise, but that he would not take Hector along.

Hector paused for an instant in his favorite occupation of "pointing" the cat, as she dozed on the hearth, and he stared fixedly at his master. But none of the people in the room had any idea the collie understood what Hogg was talking about.

Next morning at sunrise Hogg started out. Before going, he looked for Hector in order to shut him in the house. But he could not find the collie anywhere, nor did Hector come at his loudest call.

Hogg made the long trip, and at last neared Bowerhope. As he rounded a turn in the road he saw a collie dog sitting on the top of a wayside bank, placidly waiting for Hogg to come up to him. The dog was Hector.

He had started for Bowerhope, ahead of Hogg, and had swum a river swollen with spring floods in order to get there. At the end of the way, he found by his sense of scent that his master had not yet arrived. So he trotted up to the top of the high bank overlooking the road, and sat there, patiently waiting for him. Hector had heard his master's talk of the proposed trip, and had understood. Moreover, he had determined to go along.

PADDY

A Mongrel, but a Great Little Dog

SHE was white, with big yellowish blotches strewn here and there from nose to tail. She came to us when she was perhaps two months old. At that time she was as broad as she was long. Later she was to straighten out into a shapely dog that weighed about thirty pounds. Because her pudgy body and her funny wrinkled face reminded me strongly of a queer-looking chap who had been my dragoman in Greece many years earlier, we gave the new puppy the dragoman's name, which was Papadapoulos. Naturally such a double mouthful of a name was far too huge for a tiny dog. So we shortened it to Paddy. And Paddy she remained for the rest of her eight years of life.

While she was still a waddling pup, she gave first sign of the odd character that was hers. This she did by gathering mouthfuls of flowers from the meadows or the borders and carrying them gravely into the house and laying them on the floor at the feet of the first person she happened to find. As long as she brought in only wild flowers, it seemed an amusing trick. But when she was so encouraged by our laughter that she began to bite off roses and irises and lilies and other carefully-tended blooms, the habit had to be broken.

I sprinkled a very little red pepper on one or two of the flowers that grew nearest the house. Soon afterward, Paddy bit off the head of one of these—a fat June rose—and started indoors with it. Midway she halted, dropped the rose from her mouth, glared at it in cold fury for an instant, and walked away sneezing. Never again did she pick another flower.

A Mongrel, but a Great Little Dog

Her next stunt was concerned with the barn kittens. She would pick up each of these half-grown cats in turn, run wildly in an enormous circle with it, set it down unhurt, and pick up the next. One after another the four kittens would be treated to this ride. Oddly enough, the kittens seemed to enjoy the experience of being held thus lightly by the nape of the neck and carried at express train speed. Not only did they fail to resent it, but they would trot out of the stable whenever Paddy came near, and rub against her legs as if coaxing for another ride.

Paddy used to snarl hideously at a peacock we had here at Sunnybank, and the peacock would hiss at her in fury. Then they would stand face to face in fighting attitudes for perhaps a minute. After that, side by side, they would go for a solemn walk around the place. They used to cuddle down together in the shade of an arbor, for their noonday naps in hot weather. Yet every day when they met, the snarling and hissing would be repeated.

The dog was our constant companion when we went boating or driving or walking. She proved herself more than a mere comrade one day when the Mistress was walking through the woods, with Paddy at her heels. A big and ill-tempered female dog, twice Paddy's size, confronted them midway in a narrow path, and growled menacingly as the Mistress tried to walk past. The big dog snapped viciously at the Mistress, as the latter's skirt brushed lightly against her. Instantly, Paddy went into action. Screeching and ki-yi-ing as if she was in dire terror, she flashed past the Mistress and flung herself at the dog.

Less than a second later, Paddy jumped back, still screeching. She jumped back, and stood, with her lithe body guarding the Mistress. But there was no further need for guarding. In that second of whirlwind charge, Paddy had torn out the throat of the larger dog.

A Mongrel, but a Great Little Dog

I made inquiries, then, as to our queer dog's ancestry. She had been given us by a country neighbor. Now he told me that her mother had been a purebred blue-ribbon bull terrier, her sire an overgrown fox terrier of doubtful pedigree. So Paddy came honestly by her terrible prowess as a fighter, though even yet I can't understand why she ki-yi-ed as if in mortal fright, when she attacked her foe.

Twice after that Paddy got into fights, both times with dogs of her own sex and much bigger than she. Both times she screeched in that same panic-stricken way. Both times the fight lasted for barely a second. Both times the other dog's throat was torn out.

She would have been a fortune to anyone who cared for the rotten professional sport of dog-fighting, for she had a genius for ring-generalship. Our collie, Sunnybank Lad, was young in those days. He and Paddy used to romp together on the lawn, and always, by brilliant knowledge of leverage and of balance, she could trip up Laddie and throw him heavily.

When she was about a year old her first and only puppy was born. We named him Rex. His sire was a collie. By some whim of nature he grew almost to the size of a Great Dane.

Paddy was a great little pal, but she was an utter failure as a mother. Before Rex was weaned, she seemed to take a violent dislike to him. Never again would she go near him or allow him near her. She would sneak away in disgust when anyone patted or spoke to Rex.

We had begun to raise collies on a more extensive scale. Moreover, we were to be away from Sunnybank for some months, so I gave Paddy to a family that lived about three miles from here. The next day she was back at Sunnybank, having broken her chain. I was not here, but my superintendent sent her again to her new owners. Three times that

A Mongrel, but a Great Little Dog

winter, Paddy broke loose again and came home, only to be sent back.

Then her owners moved away to a town fifteen miles distant. While a yard was fixed for Paddy to live in, she was tied to a post. She yanked at the post till it broke. Then, across fifteen miles of unknown country, she started for Sunnybank, dragging the heavy post behind her. She had to swim a rather swift river and she had to swim Pompton Lake—she who hated the water—and she had to lug that big post. But she kept on.

I was writing late that night, when I heard a thumping on the veranda and then a scratching at the door and an eager whine. I opened the door. Paddy leaped upon me, yelling and dancing crazily with joy and trying to lick my face. The post still dragged behind her. I sent a check to her owners in payment for the gallant little dog. And Paddy stayed on here at Sunnybank happily for the rest of her life.

 www.ingramcontent.com/pod-product-compliance
Lightning Source LLC
Chambersburg PA
CBHW080640170426
43200CB00015B/2902